LIVING ON THE FRINGE

Living on the Fringe

A Memoir by Abraham Entin

STEINERBOOK | 2018

STEINERBOOKS

An imprint of Anthroposophic Press, Inc.
610 Main St., Great Barrington, MA 01230
www.steinerbooks.org

Printed in the United States of America

LIBRARY OF CONGRESS CONTROL NUMBER: 2018955587
ISBN: 978-1-62148-235-2 (paperback)
ISBN: 978-1-62148-236-9 (ebook)

CONTENTS

PROLOGUE

On a typically dark day of early March 1969, I sat in Chicago's Federal Courtroom, waiting to be sentenced on three counts of selling drugs.

The good news was that the drug was LSD, which had not yet been reclassified as a felony drug. I had only committed a misdemeanor.

The bad news was that they had me on three counts.

Chicago was not a good place to be a longhaired hippie. Richard Nixon had been elected president on a "law and order" platform. In another courtroom, down one floor from mine, the Chicago Seven were on trial for their part in the events surrounding the Democratic Party Convention in August 1968. They had begun as the Chicago Eight, but Bobby Seale of the Black Panther Party had his case severed from the others and stood alone, bound, shackled and convicted of contempt of court. The other seven were soon convicted of "conspiracy to incite a riot," but all charges were ultimately reversed on appeal.

Our crimes had been carried out at the same time and place, and now so were our trials, although mine had a lot less media attention. I had not cut my hair or shaved my beard, and even though my crimes had been misdemeanors, I was still a dangerous radical in the eyes of the judge.

In the midst of this scene, my parents handed me an envelope and asked me to read the contents. In the year and a half since my graduation from an elite university, I had gone from a scholarship to Yale law to being a convicted drug dealer. Surely my life was at its low point. I opened the envelope. It was a letter from my older brother. In it, he pointed out that my first name, Edward, meant "keeper of the family fortune," while my middle name, Joel, meant "prophet of doom." He suggested that it was time I started living up to my first name and stopped acting out my middle one. My parents looked at me expectantly. I crumpled up the letter and threw it into the wastebasket. It took a couple of years to happen, but at that moment I knew I had to change my name.

ACKNOWLEDGMENTS

I owe debts of gratitude to many individuals who contributed to this memoir.

First and foremost to my wife Rachael Flug for her abiding love and support, her enthusiasm for this project, and her careful and cogent editing, which helped me immeasurably.

To my son Jonas for his editing and extremely helpful suggestions on organization and presentation.

To my two wonderful daughters, Jubilee and Joanna, for their encouragement through the years.

To Dani Berleson and the members of the Senior Memoir Writing Workshop, who heard the work as it unfolded.

To Sarah Dreilich for her editing skills and publisher searches.

Finally, to my Red-haired Angel, the Lady on the Bus, and all the others I have encountered on this long and winding road.

And especially to Trevor Ravenscroft, who was there when we needed him.

"If I Can't Dance,
I Don't Want To Be Part of Your Revolution."
Emma Goldman

"...in the long run, one can't satisfactorily say no to war,
violence, and injustice unless one is simultaneously
saying yes to life, love, and laughter."
David Dellinger

"To live outside the law you must be honest..."
Bob Dylan

PART I

DUCK AND COVER

I came into the world on April 12, 1945, in a small village in the interior of Brooklyn, New York. It was a place with no name. It wasn't Carnarsie or Flatbush, East New York or Bed-Sty. It was in the Avenues named after Cities—Kingston, Albany, Troy, Schenectady, and Utica. It was on a street called "St. John's Place," which sounds like a little lane, but had an electric streetcar that drove down the middle. A few blocks from Eastern Parkway, but a whole lot less expensive. My neighborhood was, though of course I didn't know this at the time, a neighborhood "in transition."

What that meant, in 1945–50, was that black people were moving into a neighborhood that had been all white. "White flight" had not come fully to fruition, especially for people like us, on the lower steps of the economic ladder. My father, Jacob (everyone called him Jack) had dropped out of high school during the Depression. He supported his elderly mother who hardly spoke English. His father, also an East European Jewish immigrant, had started a bottle cap manufacturing business with his brother-in-law Charlie that went under in only a few months after its founding My grandfather Abraham immediately died of a cerebral hemorrhage, leaving my father, as the oldest boy, responsible for the family.

It was a family full of secrets. I did not know until I was a teenager that Jack had a younger brother and sister. His sister was developmentally disabled and institutionalized at a young age. I never learned any details about her. My Uncle Bernie, on the other hand, was my father's brilliant younger brother. Everyone hoped that Bernie would become an attorney and help to reestablish the family. He had other ideas. He became a union organizer and was active in the Communist Party. When the democratically elected government of Spain was overthrown in a military coup led by Francisco Franco, and supported by the fascist governments of Italy and Germany, Uncle Bernie immediately volunteered for the Abraham Lincoln Battalion and left for Spain. He told his family he was going to study in Paris, but my father knew, even as he watched him board the ship, that his destination was the Spanish Civil War. Like many other untrained and ill-equipped volunteers, he was dead within weeks of climbing over the Pyrenees. His body was never found, and people in the family liked to think that he was whisked away by the Russians (because of his brilliance) before he could be killed. However, witnesses later confirmed his death in an ambulance bombed by the Fascist air force. He was 23 years old when he died. His name is inscribed on the memorial in San Francisco, in the park opposite the Ferry Building, steps from where Occupy San Francisco had its encampment in 2011.

I knew none of this when growing up in Brooklyn. I didn't know we were poor, but I did know that Negroes were wealthy. They lived on Hampton Place, the small, tree-lined street opposite our Tenement apartment on St. John's Place. The only birthday party I went to as a young child was a catered affair in a social hall, with clowns and singers and dancers. The birthday boy was a Negro classmate. All of this was neither here nor there to me. I had friends and classmates of all kinds. We played stickball, punch ball, and scully. We played hide-and-seek in large groups. I can remember once hiding on the roof of a building across the street.

Both my parents worked. I walked to PS 167 on Utica Ave and Eastern Parkway with my older brother and children from the block. The parents who were home after school watched over us. There was a time I chased a ball into the street and almost got hit. Within minutes of coming home from work my parents knew the whole story.

On Fridays after school I took the streetcar to my maternal grandparent's apartment, where the whole family gathered for Shabbas dinner. I was allowed to take the streetcar, but I was supposed to ask a grown-up to help me across St. John's Place after I got off. I never did.

My Bubby (Yiddish for grandmother) was a much beloved figure in our family. She was kind to everyone and was a great cook. She never learned to read or write a word of English, although she had been in the country since she was a girl. She traveled all over New York by (we believed) memorizing the number of subway stops until hers and recognizing landmarks around the city. She lived to be over 100 years old.

My mother was the eldest child of her family. Everyone called her brother "Jay," to differentiate him from my father who shared his name. He worked in the fashion industry in Manhattan in a high stress environment. He was small and always looked younger than his years, so he grew a mustache to add some age and dignity to his demeanor. He would

tell my brother and I and his two sons, Arthur and Ron-
nie, stories about "Velvull the Volf" and his adventures. He
always seemed full of fun and we stayed close all our lives.
As I write he is approaching his hundredth birthday with his
mind intact, but his body failing, in the Jewish Home for the
Aging in Miami. Jay moved down to Miami after he retired
and volunteered at the facility. Later he gave them a substantial donation that entitled him to life care at the Home when
and if it became necessary. The family likes to joke that he is
the only one who ever made money on this investment—far
outliving the value of the donation he gave.

I asked Jay, after he had moved to Florida, how he had
been able to retire so early. He explained to me that as the
piece-goods and trim buyer, he had been courted by salesmen
from many companies. "Buttons are buttons," he explained,
so whoever left the best "envelope" for him got the order.
The money, of course, was put into a secret account that the
IRS never saw.

Life in the Shmata business-or the "rag trade" as it is
called in English.

Life was a lot harder for our Jack. He had been in the coal
business during the war. Family legend had it that my mother
did not allow him to participate in the Black Market opportunities available, but whether it was this, fear or patriotism,
the war ended with him as poor as when it began. He drove
a taxi for awhile and then went to work as a driver-salesman
for the FF&V cookie company. This was a union shop, with
routes assigned by seniority, and it would take years for him
to get a route that would bring a decent living. When I was
seven, my father heard that the Stella D'oro Biscuit Company
in the Bronx was looking to expand to Chicago. If he were

willing to go there, he would have Route #2 instead of Route #1002 at FFV. My father moved to Chicago to see if it would work. He stayed with distant cousins and came home a couple of times before my mother, brother and I left our native village and made the internal migration to a whole new life in what was, to us, Another Country.

There were three incidents from these early years in Brooklyn that had a decisive influence on my later life. The first involved my friend Robbie.

Even though we all played together as a group, it is natural for children to feel a closer affinity to one or two others. Robbie was one of those boys to me. Even so, in the rough and tumble of neighborhood life, arguments and disagreements happen. In one particular case, we ended up exchanging blows. Robbie went home and I did not see him for several days. When I asked my parents what had happened to him, they explained that he had a problem with his heart and was resting in bed. I was sure that I had hurt him badly. It was the last fight I ever had. Robbie was okay (although he did have a rheumatic heart and died relatively young), but I understood that violence was not something I was willing to engage in.

The second incident happened on the way to school.

One morning when I was walking to school with my brother and his friends, one of them asked me who my "guard" was. (First and second graders came into the auditorium in the morning and were watched over by a "guard" from an higher grade who led them to their classrooms.) I replied that my guard was a girl named Anita. Anita was black. I had trouble pronouncing "R's" at that age, so it came out that Anita was my "god." One of the boys started laughing and saying that "Eddie has a nigger god." The others joined in. I knew they were making fun of me, but I also knew they were saying something nasty about Anita as well. I remember thinking, "boy, do I not want to be like them."

Before I go on, I should explain that "Edward" was my birth name in English. My Hebrew name was Avraham/ Abraham, after my father's father. In those days Jewish parents did not want to saddle their child with an obviously Jewish name, so they gave me the name of an English King instead. I never felt comfortable with that name (except for a short time when I fancied myself "Fast Eddie" after Paul Newman's pool shark character in *The Hustler*), but it took me until I was 26 years old and living in California to shed that moniker and take the name Abraham back for myself.

The third incident was more ongoing.

In 1950, when I started school, it was at the height of the Cold War. The Russians had got the Atomic Bomb. Fall-out shelters and Civil Defense were at their peak. At PS 167, this translated into Air Raid Drills to supplement the Fire Drills that were part of school life.

Since we were part of New York City, even though we lived in Brooklyn, we were likely targets for attack. In the event of such an attack we were trained to duck under our desks and cover our heads to keep us safe from the bombs dropping in the streets or on our school.

One day, in midst of this drill, I looked up from under my desk at the plate glass windows above me. In that moment, I understood that there was no way ducking and covering was going to keep me safe from the bombs that might drop. And that was immediately followed by the question, "Don't they know that? Don't the teachers and the principal and all the adults telling us to do this know that it's useless? " And I immediately felt that there was nothing these people in authority could teach me.

This feeling was reinforced by two other factors. The first was that, with my father away in Chicago and my mother working full time, there were no authority figures close to me. My father's mother had lived with us, but she was old and meant nothing to me. When my father moved to Chicago, she moved into an old people's home and out of our apartment. My older brother had his own life and little interest in mine. So, for that year between seven and eight, I was essentially on my own.

I was in third grade. My teacher, Miss Maryland, was a witch. She was mean and clearly did not like children. Her passion as a teacher was cursive handwriting and we spent hours working on this every class. I refused to learn it. I just wouldn't do it. And, in fact, I never learned to write legibly. Even today I can't read my own handwriting.

My relationship to authority was set during that year. I did not trust adults—especially those who tried to tell me what to do. I knew I was smarter than they were and that I was going to have to figure things out for myself. I was going to be the boss of me.

SIXTEEN TONS

When we got to Chicago in the summer of 1953, we stayed with the cousins my father had boarded with before we arrived. They lived on the West Side of Chicago and were pretty much the last white people in the neighborhood.

Chicago's West Side was a huge black ghetto. Block after block after block of rundown apartments and poor looking people. All my ideas about Negroes being rich went out the window. I didn't understand words like "block busting" or "white flight" yet, but on some level I understood that my impression of Negroes as "richer than us" needed revision.

Racism was just part of the air in Chicago. It was the most segregated city in the country. Lots of

Irish, Italian, Polish, Greeks, Jews—everybody had their neighborhood and all were united to keep black people out. There was nothing subtle about it. The year we arrived in Chicago was the year Richard Daley was elected Mayor. Chicago had its local elections during odd years, as it was easier for the Machine to control a smaller turnout than a larger one. Daley was Mayor when I left Chicago in 1970, and only his death made me realize someone not named Daley could be Mayor. At least for a while—until Richard II took over the throne.

I had only gotten a glimpse of racism back in Brooklyn. Now, in Chicago, that kind of casual and pervasive racism was all around me, even though the neighborhood we settled into was on the North Side, where no black people lived.

We moved into an apartment at 546 Addison Street. It was a third-story apartment, but there was only one other apartment on our floor. We had bay windows and a walk-in pantry in the kitchen. What we did not have was a bedroom for me, and I continued to share a room with my older brother—a condition that did not change until I went to college.

The apartment was only a block from Lincoln Park and Lake Michigan at the east end. There was no beach at our part of the park, but we could dive off the rocks if we were brave enough.

The street next to the park was Lake Shore Drive, or "The Drive" as it was called. There were already a few high-rise luxury apartment buildings, but the real development of the street was just beginning. I learned to ride a bicycle in an empty lot that became a tall building within a few years.

Because we arrived in Chicago early in the summer, school was already out and there were no groups of children playing on the street. I was alone in a way I had never been before. My mother met the man who owned the newsstand on the corner. He was Jewish and had a son my age who would be in my class at LeMoyne School in the Fall. We were brought together to play and I was told to "make friends" with him. I had no idea what that meant. In Brooklyn, everyone played together and friendships grew out of this continual interaction. I missed my neighborhood, my Bubby and my aunt and uncle. I felt very much alone, and my mother felt the same way. She continually referred to Chicago as a "hick town" and missed her family tremendously. She ultimately came to love Chicago and her life there, but those first few years were very hard on her.

Starting school in the fall was an even greater change for me. I cannot remember ever reading or being able to read while living in Brooklyn. Now, in fourth grade, we were given "reading units" to complete. We were assigned to read three- to four-page stories and answer questions at the end, so that the teacher knew we had read the unit and understood it. I could read anything. I completed unit after unit—more than twice as many as anyone else in the class. When we were given a standardized test later in the year, they said I could read at a ninth-grade level—unheard of for a fourth grader. I don't know how it happened, and I certainly don't remember "learning" to read. I could just do it.

I discovered the public library a half-mile from my house. I read all of the Landmark books as they came out. The series had begun in 1951 and were about American history (later adding world history as well). My parents gave me the book *They All Are Jews*, which consisted of short bios of famous Jews who had an impact on the world. Einstein, of course, was the climax of the book. But Marx and Trotsky were in there, too.

The Hardy Boys and Nancy Drew quickly led to the great Nero Wolfe series, and a lifetime love of detective fiction. After I got a bicycle, I would ride down to the library at least once a week, carrying way too many books in both directions. No one told me what to read. I made my own choices and continued the process of self-education I had begun under the desk during the duck and cover exercises at P.S. 167.

Even though I loved to read and was very good at school, I was determined not to be seen as a "bookworm." I loved sports, and was good enough not to be the last picked. I played baseball, football, dodge ball, and any other ball that was available. I adapted to the 16-inch softball played in Chicago, and later made the football team as a freshman in high school. I was, however, secretly delighted that the practices conflicted with Honor Classes, and that my parents insisted I not join the team. For a change, I did not argue with them. I also played poker, gin, pinochle and blackjack—for money whenever possible.

It was mostly my irreverent attitude towards authority that kept me from "Bookworm" status. I spent much of sixth grade sitting outside the classroom because of my continual joking and disruption of the lessons. The classroom was right next to that of my fifth grade teacher, Mrs. Goldberg, who had been very proud of my academic prowess. She always saw me sitting outside, and would shake her head in disappointment.

At the end of fifth grade our class had been split. Those in the "honors" group were moved into a class that was half 6A and half 6B. At Christmas break we were all promoted to seventh grade. This made me even younger than my classmates—I was already younger because the deadlines for starting school were different in New York and Chicago, so I would have started school later in Chicago. Now I was 18 months younger than the others in my class. Any time my parents told me I was "too young" to do something, I would respond that my classmates did it, and it wasn't my choice to be the youngest. If they wanted me to act my age, I could fail a few grades and move backwards. Otherwise, I wanted the perks of my grade. They took the deal.

I also tried to help other people. I had started an "Archaeology Club" in sixth grade, when we were studying Ancient History. This soon morphed into "The Polio Club," where we raised funds for the March of Dimes and for UNICEF on Halloween. We talked about current events and tried to figure out what was going on in the world.

Seventh and eight grade were the best of my academic life—until graduate school at UCLA, but that is another story. In seventh grade we got Miss Stollberg, the youngest teacher in the school. She was pretty and funny, but also had a fearsome reputation as a disciplinarian. The legend was that she had started off nice, but kids thought they could take advantage of her and so she got hard, and fast. Our class was a mix of smart, mostly Jewish kids who had "skipped" into the class and the more working class kids we had joined. All white, of course. But there was one Puerto Rican guy who was not quite 16 so had to be in school, and had been put into seventh grade because Miss Stollberg was the only one who was not scared of him. Orlando was almost six feet tall and looked way older than sixteen. He wore a ducktail haircut and sat in the back of the class whacking a ruler against his penis, which seemed to go all the way to his knee. The rumor was that he had three children, but no one was going to ask him about it.

Miss Stollberg was the teacßher who gave a few of us a copy of *The Catcher in the Rye*. It was one of the things great teachers did during those years. I spent a good portion of the year under her desk, where she could hit me with her ruler if I got too rowdy. We would come back to see her all the time, even in high school and after she got married and became Mrs. Legator. She and my mother ran into each other over the years, and she always asked about me.

In eighth grade we had the anti-Stollberg; Elsie Barlow was the senior teacher in the school. She was very old and we unkindly called her "Elsie the Cow" after a well-known advertising symbol of the era. Her brothers had fought in World War I and she loved to lead us in patriotic songs. Her favorite was "Over There." We also sang "The Marine Hymn" and all the other military anthems.

The principal, Mrs. Lawrence, was on leave finishing up her Doctorate. Miss Barlow became acting principal, which kept her out of the classroom a lot. She explained all this to us and then said that the President of the class would be in charge when she was gone, and it was up to us to elect that person. I called a meeting of the boys and said that it was very important to elect one of us as president, that we should have an election among ourselves and agree beforehand we would all vote for the winner. They chose me. I won the general election by one vote—the girl I ran against voted for me out of courtesy, and I voted for myself because I wanted to win. Girls have become a lot less courteous since those days.

I was in charge. Within a few weeks we were playing football with a miniature ball in the hallways. The whole thing came crashing down several weeks later. We all agreed to steal a cigarette from our parents and bring it to school to smoke. While we were doing this, one of the girls ran down to the office to tell on us. By the time Elsie came into the class, the cigarettes were gone. She made us do what her mother had made her brothers do when they smoked—kiss her on the mouth so she could smell their breath. Then she sent notes home to our parents and required that they come to school. The end of my political career had come.

In 1955 a song came out that took the pop charts by storm. It was an unexpected crossover hit from country music. During that time there were a number of evening fifteen-minute television shows that featured different singers. I first heard Nat King Cole this way. He was just about the only black person on television. I don't know if I realized at the time that his show had no commercials—nobody would sponsor a black performer. Another show was with a guy called "Tennessee Ernie Ford." He was a homey, down-south type who sang country music. His cover of "Sixteen Tons" was playing everywhere. It was about the life of a coal miner, and the chorus went:

> You load sixteen tons and what do you get
> Another day older and deeper in debt
> St. Peter don't you call me 'cause I can't go
> I owe my soul to the company store.

My father wasn't a coal miner; he was a truck driver. But I watched him and my mom argue over putting tomatoes in the salad during the winter and struggle to make ends meet, leaving their birthplace just to make a living—the words spoke right to my feelings about our lives. It was, and still is, a perfect description of life for the working person delivered in four short lines. From "Sixteen Tons" it was a short step to Woody Guthrie, Pete Seeger and, later, Dylan as the sources for information about how the world around us was ruled and directed.

I started a rock band in 1958. We named ourselves "Fats Entin and the Dynamos." Our signature song was "Blueberry Hill." Roy Johnson delivered "Great Balls of Fire" and dreamboat Ricky Garcia played electric guitar. I was the passionate lead singer who could not carry a tune. We had a good time. There were 'tween dances at the synagogue and we could dance to "At the Hop" and even some doo-wop. Black and white musics were coming together in new ways and the jitterbug was the dance of the day.

There were a lot of parties, big bar mitzvahs for the wealthier kids and lots of birthday parties, as well. We had started playing kissing games like spin the bottle. At one of those parties I found myself making out on a bed covered with winter coats. We were snuggled beneath them. I felt myself stirring in a way that I had never experienced before. Then someone came in and said it was time to go.

I got home about an hour later than I was supposed to, but my parents were not back from wherever they had gone. I could not sleep. When they finally returned home, I tried to tell them about what had happened at the party and how I was feeling. Perhaps they were tired or embarrassed, but instead of answering my questions they focused on the fact that I had stayed out an hour later than I was supposed to. Once again I experienced the feeling of being on my own, and that the adults around me would be of no help in figuring out how to navigate the world.

Then came high school.

MOST LIKELY TO SUCCEED

For some of us, high school is the highlight of our lives. We are big fish in a small pond. The prettiest girl, who dreams of being a movie star and finds out soon enough that there are lots of other prettiest girls who have the same dream. Or the star player who is not good enough to get an athletic scholarship to the State U and starts working at the local garage. It is certainly an old and oft-told American tale.

Then there are the Nerds. The geeky boys, picked on by the popular and athletic, snubbed by the girls, who later start big companies and become stars of the new economy. Also an old American folk tale.

It didn't take long for me to be shown my place in the new setting of high school. It began with my Bar Mitzvah.

Everyone in my neighborhood—all the Jewish kids—got bar mitzvahed. Some learned their Haftorah part via a record that they memorized. Others went to Hebrew School and Sunday School and learned how to read the Haftorah—which is the commentary on the Bible reading of the week. I was among that group.

I hated Hebrew school. I understood before my Bar Mitzvah that I had no choice in going, whether I liked it or not. It wasn't a battle I could win, like the one about age-appropriateness.

My brother went to Hebrew School in Brooklyn until his bar-mitzvah, and so would I and so would my cousins back in Brooklyn. It didn't matter what the other kids might or might not do. There was no negotiating this one.

I was the last in my class and crowd to be bar mitvahed and the only one bar mitzvahed in high school. Almost all the receptions were at hotels or halls, rented for the occasion, and catered. Also a band, and you got to stay out late and dance. Mine was at our apartment. Relatives came from New York and the local cousins were there. Of the classmates invited, some came and some did not. And some who did come forgot to bring a gift. It was a clear message that I was out, made even clearer when I was not invited into the "cool Jew" social club on campus. No one was ever nasty to me—they knew my mouth, and that I wasn't afraid to use it—they just weren't my friends any more. Welcome to the wonderful world of high school.

It didn't help that our school, Lake View High, was a square block-brick building that opened directly onto the street. We walked from class to class in what looked and felt like a prison. The freshman boys had gym class first thing in the morning and had to swim and shower naked in a group. Everything about it felt like a prison, and the warden was a notorious anti-Semite.

The freshman girls were now the targets of upperclassmen guys. No more parties. The clubs had "mixers," but since I was not in a club there was just no way to meet girls. There were three of us "working class Jews" who had come to high school together and found ourselves in the same isolated position. We shared our misery and tried to find a way out of our situation.

Classes were a complete bore. Even the honors classes did nothing to stimulate or teach me anything. I found myself reading a library book inside my textbook during class. I did learn to take advantage of study hall periods to actually do my schoolwork. In four years of high school I never took a book home or did any homework outside of school hours. Still, the hours spent in school were interminable and I spent most of my days during the first two years staring at the clock and fantasizing about the unattainable girls around me.

These high school years, from 1958–62, were filled with frightening events in the outside world. It was the height of the cold war. The Berlin Wall went up, and the "Doomsday Clock" of the Union of Concerned Scientists hovered between 5 and 1 minute to midnight. I remember myself at lunch hour, eating off-campus at the local hamburger joint and discussing how to steal my father's car and escape to Alaska, where the fallout was (we thought) less likely to kill us. The fact that none of us could drive or had the money for gas did not seem to play into our calculations.

One of the girls from our grammar school group was named Leslie. Leslie's family was different from the rest of ours. Her parents did something "artistic" and they were much cooler than anyone else's parents. Leslie was a good friend. She was rather tall for her age and somewhat awkward through eighth grade. As soon as she got into high school, she blossomed and became, by far, the prettiest girl at Lake View. She began going out with friends of her older brother, who was a senior. By our sophomore year she was dating college guys, but was still our friend and classmate at Lake View.

One day, Leslie asked me to sign a petition against nuclear arms. It was being circulated by the Student Peace Union (SPU), which was a youth group sponsored by the Communist Party of American. I told her that I could not sign it as it might affect my chances of getting into Law School. She expressed her disappointment and said, "You're a better person than that."

I went home and thought about what she had said— what she had asked me to do and how I had responded. I had no illusion that signing the petition would get me a date with Leslie, but I did care what she thought of me, and I certainly agreed that ending nuclear weapons would be a good idea. Was I really going to be more concerned with how somebody at a law school seven years from now might view my actions than someone I liked and respected now? Did I really want to live my life trying to please people I did not know and would probably not even like, because they could affect my future?

The next day at school I found Leslie and signed her petition. If this was going to keep me out of law school, then perhaps law school was not the place for me.

Of course, everyone knew that I was going to become a lawyer. I was a very smart Jewish boy. I was not good at or interested in Science, so being a doctor was out. The only thing going for me in that department was my terrible handwriting. I didn't particularly like Math, although I was okay in the subject, but no one, including myself, could see me as a CPA. That, plus my big mouth, left everyone convinced that being a lawyer was to be my profession and path in life. I took Latin as my foreign language because so many legal terms came from there. I joined the debate club and argued with everyone and anyone. This was who I was and was going to be.

That summer, during my second year of high school, I went back to New York for a visit. I could stay with my Aunt Huddy and my Bubbie, who had moved to Queens from their old place in Brooklyn. I went to Brighton Beach with a couple of friends from my old neighborhood and also saw my cousins. One of my older cousins on my father's side was named Muriel. Her father, my Uncle Charlie, was married to my father's Aunt Lena. Aunt Lena and Uncle Charlie had an apartment in Long Beach that they rented every summer. I had learned to swim in the ocean on my visits there. Uncle Charlie had been a partner with my grandfather Abraham in the bottle cap factory they had opened right before the depression hit. When the factory went under and Abraham died of his cerebral hemorrhage, Charlie went to work selling bottle caps for someone else. Charlie always greeted me by asking "So, how's business?" He also taught me to play gin rummy, a skill that served me well during my college years.

Charlie and Lena had two daughters. The daughters hated each other for some reason unknown to us younger children, but often got into drunken brawls at big family functions. My father's family was rift with these kinds of family feuds that no one would explain to us kids.

Muriel, the younger daughter, was an interior decorator by trade. She was flamboyant and loved to be avant-garde and shocking. It was during this visit in the summer of 1959 that Muriel told me about my Uncle Bernie and his death in Spain.

All of this came as a complete shock and revelation to me. My parents were very upset with Muriel, who they felt had no business telling this to me. My parents worried that Bernie could become a romantic role model. They understood the power relationships in society, but they were focused on surviving these conditions, not on changing them. They had seen through Bernie and others, how dangerous that could be, and hoped I would stay off that path. They would have been more than happy if I had never heard his name.

A year or so later, my mother took me shopping for clothes. By this time my father was doing better financially, and my mother was working as well. She was always happier when she had a job and a life outside of the house, and I was, too. On this occasion, we were shopping for a winter coat. We came upon a beautiful leather jacket. Not a big, thick one, but rather a stylish black jacket with very soft leather. The salesman, trying to close the deal, said that it was made of the finest Spanish leather. I immediately put it back and said that I could never wear a coat made in a fascist country that had killed my uncle and would buy nothing from Spain until it was a democracy again. My mother gave me a strange and worried look, but she did not argue. We bought something else, and I never found a jacket that nice. Every time I heard Bob Dylan sing "Spanish Boots of Spanish Leather," I would remember that moment.

As I progressed through high school I began to develop strategies for dealing with the mind-numbing boredom and the social isolation. One of these strategies was to find ways to miss or get out of school. I joined the Key Club not only as a way to bolster my extra-curriculum resume for college, but also because one could attend some of the monthly Kiwanis Luncheons and miss a half day of school. At one of these, in 1960, they had a screening of a film called "Operation

Abolition." It was an expose of the awful conduct by students in Berkeley who were disrupting the House Un-American Activities Committee hearings at the University. I watched with fascination as the camera followed students sliding down the banister and generally disrupting the hearings with laughter and ridicule. I had a hard time keeping a straight face as the Kiwanis members recoiled in horror at the behavior of these unruly and disobedient students. I loved them from the get-go, and found myself meeting many of them years later when I came to California.

I began to bring Jim Beam whiskey to school in a cough medicine bottle. I would take a walk during lunch and spend the afternoon quietly drunk in the classroom. When I turned sixteen I got a work permit. I scheduled lunch and a study period right before last period and was able to leave school by noon every day.

I also spent a lot of time gambling. We played poker for higher stakes than we could afford, and always owed each other more than could be paid. We also played a high stakes variation of blackjack called "Pot Luck." We spent a lot of time and energy finding places to play almost every day after school. Even though much of the money was on account (on account of we had less than we were betting), some cash was necessary for this and other teenage needs.

My friends Sheldon and Burton and I were asked to check coats at the Friday night services at the Synagogue. This was Chicago, and people wore heavy coats during the winter. We were paid $5 or $10 per week for this. During the service we would hang out in the community center with the janitors. We would give them money to buy a bottle (usually Jim Beam) and they would share it with us. Somehow we managed to get congregants their right coats back, but I am not sure how. The main thing, however, was that by doing this we got to do the coat checking for fairs and other big events at the Synagogue. We got paid, and there was also a tip jar. The tip jar was supposedly for the Synagogue, but we always shared well in the proceeds. We could sometimes make $20 or $30 dollars each over the weekend—a lot of money in those days, especially for kids our age.

A LITTLE LOWER THAN THE ANGELS

I stopped trying to have any social life connected with school. The synagogue had remained an important part of my life. Although I had finally left Hebrew School, I still attended Sunday School. This was made more palatable by the Sunday Morning Breakfast Club, where the Synagogue Men's Club provided bagels, cream cheese and lox, plus pastries, for the students and any fathers who wanted to join us. The teachers were younger and more involving than the older ladies who taught Hebrew School. One of the teachers was Mr. Specter He used a book in his class entitled *A Little Lower than the Angels*. I don't remember much about the content, but the title has stayed with me. It laid out the central question of my life—who are we as human beings? Are we apes with opposable thumbs or evolving spiritual beings: two diametrically different possibilities.

This is not an abstract question, even though no one can "prove" their position one way or another. It is a question that fundamentally influences how we view ourselves, other human beings and the society we live in. It is the question posed in *Lord of the Flies*, one of the most influential books of that era. Does society and its institutions exist to socialize and control the beast within us or to liberate the angel trying to be born? Is war a necessary result of "human nature," or an artificial construct of a order built upon violence and fear? These kinds of questions were first raised in Sunday school and bull sessions during high school, and continue to be important questions for me, and for us as human beings. Still, it was the social scene that was most important to me. There was a youth group at the synagogue that was part of a city wide and national group called "United Synagogue Youth." Through this I was able to meet young people from all over the city and surrounding suburbs. They knew nothing of me or my family background and could not have cared less. They took me for who I was and I began making friends among them. My parents loved that I was so active in a synagogue sponsored organization and did not mind that I spent weekends at other people's houses or attended events all over. As long as my grades were good (which they always were) I could come and go as I pleased.

I became quite well known in the organization, and friends with many of the "movers and shakers" in the group. Because of this I was put on the official slate for election of regional officers. The slate candidates always won the elections, with the backing of the adult leadership. I was slated for corresponding secretary. My opponent was a girl who had helped as a volunteer in the office and was familiar with the job. She would certainly have been a much better corresponding secretary, but I won. After the fun of the election wore off, I realized what had happened and immediately began a campaign to end the slating of candidates. This brought me into conflict with the executive director of the organization, as well as some of the other winners. I persisted and ended the practice through this campaign. I was also the worst corresponding secretary in the history of CHUSY

(Chicago United Synagogue Youth). My defeated opponent, a true saint, continued working in the office to actually get the mail to the membership.

The problem was that the stated goal of the organization was "developing leadership" among teenagers, and being on the inside had shown me that it was really the adults who were making the decisions and controlling the organization. To me it was another example of adult hypocrisy. It was also the first time that I had a chance to actually do something to confront it, and I quite naturally jumped at the chance. I found that my fellow officers were not at all interested in joining my crusade. They loved the prestige of their office and the way it looked on their college resumes and did not share my indignation about the situation. They couldn't believe I was making such a fuss, and I ended up completely isolated on the board. A couple of my colleagues were in my college class, but they avoided me like the plague.

The whole issue of "Jewish Identity" was coming to a head during these years—not just for me, but also for a whole generation of Jewish youth. The State of Israel was born only three years after I was, and the relationship between Jews in Israel and in the rest of the world was in a period of development. The Jewish community in the United States was the largest and wealthiest, and support from this community was vital for the survival of the new State. As young Jews we were naturally expected to participate in these efforts. We raised money to plant trees to help "make the desert bloom." The prevailing narrative was that Israel was "a land without people for a people without land" and "the only democracy in the Middle East." It represented a civilizing impulse in a backward part of the world. The communal farms (Kibbutzim) were a experiment in Socialism. It was all very idealistic.

One of the leading personalities in our synagogue was a man named Ben Aronin. He was an attorney, scholar, raconteur, and founder of the Breakfast club. He seemed like a sweet and gentle soul. It was a shock (to me) when, during one of the periodic Israeli–Arab conflicts he went around collecting money to buy guns to ship to Israel and spoke about killing off all the Arabs in the region.

My mother had taken a job working for the Zionist Organization in Chicago. This brought us into contact with Israeli Jews, some of whom settled in Chicago and others who came through on fundraising or political missions. They all seemed to treat American Jews as "second class"—either cash cows or cowards for not directly joining the struggle for Jewish survival. Either way, we were expected to follow their lead and support whatever they did. *Arrogant* was the word most often used, in private, to describe them.

The synagogue we belonged to was named Anshe Emet, which translates to "People of Truth." It was part of the "Conservative" Jewish Movement. There are, broadly speaking, three branches of modern Judaism—the Orthodox, the Conservative and the Reform. Of course, all three have many sub-groups within them. The joke is that if there are three Jews in the town, there will be four synagogues. There is probably the same joke about Christian Protestants.

From my perspective of more than fifty years ago, I saw the differences in this way:

The Orthodox adhere to the many laws governing daily life as described in the Bible. They interact with the modern economic world but otherwise try to remain separate. To them, the Conservative and Reform Jews are not really Jewish at all.

The Reform Jews see themselves as Jewish through blood and culture. They are embarrassed by the Orthodox and try to become as fully integrated into modern society as possible. Their worship services are in English and they do not cover their heads when praying. "You don't need to believe in God to be Jewish" is how I saw their attitude.

The Conservatives are somewhere in the middle. The Orthodox embarrass them, too, but they are not ready to abandon the religious aspects of Judaism. My mother, for instance, kept a Kosher home but would eat pork, shellfish, or any other food she wanted to in a restaurant without guilt. Conservatives are the most "agnostic" of the groupings, struggling to keep an old tradition alive in a modern world.

None of the three groupings allowed women to read from the Torah or to become Rabbis or Cantors.

Our synagogue was famous for its Cantor (the person who sings the prayers during the service). He had a very beautiful voice and was extremely handsome. He was something of a celebrity, having coached Danny Thomas for his role in the 1952 remake of *The Jazz Singer*—the first movie musical which stared Al Jolson as a cantor's son who abandons his tradition to become a popular singer, only to return at the end to his roots. A Jewish Al Green. All the women at the synagogue fawned over him. I couldn't stand him—he just made the services even longer than they had to be by going on and on with his show-off singing.

Anshe Emet had a large chapel, but also kept a smaller room for the older members who preferred a more traditional service done all in Hebrew, with no sermons or other "frills." After having a bar mitzvah, almost all of the young people stopped coming to services (except for holidays). Burton, Sheldon and I decided to join the older men in the "bet midrash." They loved having us. My father's father had died long ago and my mother's father was an old man who hardly spoke English when I knew him. He was large and somewhat crippled. He spent his days at the small synagogue next door to their apartment. My grandparents had an overhead shower in their bathroom, with a small, round shower curtain in the middle, and a wooden kitchen chair positioned underneath it. This chair was for my grandfather to sit on while Bubby bathed him. Although I never saw her doing it, I could picture it in my mind.

The old men in the bet midrash became surrogate grandfathers for me, offering warmth and joking camaraderie with older men that I had never experienced in my personal life. It kept me coming back for a year or more. I kept struggling to understand how this ancient tradition could help me understand and cope with the world I was living in. What troubled me most was the disparity between the power of the ritual and the effect—or lack there of—it had on the people practicing it. The Jewish people I knew spoke of those outside the tribe with contempt—and the more religious they were, the more contempt for "the goyim" they expressed. They hated them for what they had done to the Jews—for the centuries of persecution they had endured, but seemed to have learned little about compassion and tolerance. I understood and felt connected to the stream of Jewish social advocacy, but too many of the Jews I knew spoke about black people (*Schvartzes*) in terms reminiscent of how European Jews had been described only a decade before. There was one family gathering in particular when some of my older cousins were bad mouthing the emerging civil rights movement and I called them out on it. They told me I was "full of shit" and I swore back at them. My father overheard and came over, looked at them and said, "No, you are the ones who are full of it." We had never spoken about it before, but it meant the world to me that he had taken my side. Neither of my parents were surprised when I later became active in the Civil Rights Movement and they didn't try to stop my participation. They did, however, adamantly oppose interracial dating (or any dating outside the faith) on the grounds that "if you don't date them you won't marry them," but that was the case among all parents in those days.

Looking back, it is clear that this was a time when the attention of the American Jewish community was turning towards Israel and its interests, and away from concerns about conditions at home. As the United States became more and more Israel's "champion" and chief financial supporter, the organized Jewish leadership naturally became more reluctant to be critical of the United States and its government. For me, being Jewish was becoming more and more irrelevant to who I was and who I was becoming. It would be several more years before this process would be completed, but my estrangement from my roots was already beginning.

YOU CAN'T SAY THAT

When the school year ended in June of 1960, I had nothing to do. I wasn't going to camp and there was no job for me. My new friend, Dave Fishman from the USY group in Rogers Park, told me he was going to sell magazines door to door and invited me to join the crew.

These crews went from city to city selling subscriptions to various publications. They sold and also recruited local kids like us to fill out their crews. We were paid on a straight commission basis, with the crew chief getting a percentage of our sales. We would go from door to door offering a "free advertising gift," which, along the way, became a paid subscription to a group of magazines. There was nothing illegal about it, but it was not clear how much, if anything, one saved over a regular subscription. Still, it was something to do and seemed a likely fit for fast-talking teenagers like Dave and me.

Summer in Chicago is hot and humid, punctuated by hard rain that goes away but leaves the humidity behind. If one can stay near the Lake it is marginally better, but the suburbs north and west of Chicago are generally five to ten degrees hotter than the city itself.

On this particular day, about four weeks into my stint as a door-to-door salesman, we were dropped off in one of the developing suburbs northwest of the city. No trees, no shade, just block after block of new tract houses. We were dropped off at a gas station and told that the chief would be back in three hours to pick us up. We were all given our territories and set out to make our fortunes.

After about two hours I had just about come to the end of my territory and had sold nothing. I was hot, thirsty, and disgusted. I knocked on the door of a house just like every other. The door opened and the lady of the house appeared. I said "hi, Mam. I've got your free advertising gift for you." She looked at me and said, "You ain't got nothin' for me kid," and slammed the door in my face. I stood there and just started swearing. Not loud—I certainly didn't intend for her to hear me—but loud enough that her maid/cleaning lady, who was working near the window, could hear every word. I heard her say "You hear what that boy is callin' you!" A few seconds later the door swung open and this very large, German-looking woman fills the doorway, carrying a big broom. She looks at me with venom in her eyes and says "I'm gonna' kick your ass, you little punk" and starts swinging her broom. I turn and run and she chases me down the street, yelling and swinging. Being a fifteen-year-old boy, I was able to outrun her and make my way back to the gas station to wait an hour for the rest of the crew to return.

After about a half hour, a squad car pulls into the station. A cop gets out, walks up to me, and asks if I am part of the magazine sales crew. I say yes and look over at the car, where the lady with the broom is sitting in the back seat waving her arms wildly. The cop tells me to get into the car and he sits between her and me in the back seat. As we take off to the station, the woman looks at me and says "I'm gonna put your ass in the shithouse." I say, "Hey lady, you can get arrested for talking like that." The cop tells us both to shut up. We get to the station, where the rest of the crew is waiting. They tell us to get out of town and not come back, and they tell me that they are not going to arrest me, but they are going to call my parents.

When I got home that evening, my mother was waiting for me. She asked if anything had happened at work that day. I knew the jig was up so I told her the story. She wasn't too upset, but she said she was going to have to tell my father about this when he got home. When we sat down to dinner that night, my mother said I had something to tell him. I told him the story, wondering what my punishment might be. When I was done, he started to laugh, harder than I had ever seen him laugh before. When he stopped laughing he shook his head and said, "You gotta learn to watch your mouth, kid," and went back to his food. That was my last day as a door-to-door salesman.

My first real job was at the commissary/grocery store that opened in the new high-rise apartment building on the corner of Addison and Lake Shore Dr. I was originally hired to do stocking, but it turned out that many people would call in orders to the commissary from within the building as well as other buildings up and down LSD. The other stock clerks and I ended up spending most of our time pushing shopping carts around the neighborhood delivering groceries. Almost every delivery included a quarter tip—sometimes a half a buck, if it was a big order or a generous customer. We often stopped in the building delivery room to gamble our quarters with the guys who delivered UPS and Post Office packages within the building and who also got lots of quarter tips. We would toss our coins in the air and call heads or tails. One of us would pick up the heads and the other the tails. During one of these sessions my boss walked in and saw the coins in the air. "When you finish picking those up, come and pick up your paycheck." That was the end of my first job.

During the summer of 1961, between the first and second parts of twelfth grade, I worked as a kitchen boy at camp Avodah in Michigan. *Avodah* means "work" in Hebrew. The camp came out of the Labor/Zionist Movement, which had spawned the Kibbutz communities in Israel. It had been founded to foster a love for work among the campers, but by the time I got there it was pretty much like any summer camp, but with a Jewish clientele and atmosphere.

As a kitchen boy I helped prepare meals for more than 200 campers and staff. The cooks were two black men who had been cooks in the Navy, and who ran a tight ship in the kitchen. We worked fast and we worked hard. When mealtime was over we were staff with no responsibility for campers. We could play basketball, swim, read, or just hang out until the next mealtime came around. It was a perfect job for me and I learned a skill that has stood me in good stead for the rest of my life.

Summer camps are great centers of sexual intrigue and activity. Warm summer nights, minimal adult supervision, and lots of opportunity to sneak off for some fun. I was one of the youngest staff members, so the junior counselors and oldest campers were most available to me. One of the campers was a smart, beautiful, and sweet girl named Karen. Karen was just entering high school, and even though I was attracted to her, I just could not overcome the age difference. She ended up with my best friend at camp, Alan Winter, who was a year younger than me. The three of us hung out together a lot and they made a wonderful couple. I went after one of the junior counselors, an older girl with a reputation for being "fast." We spent much of the summer making out, with me trying desperately to take things to the next level, and her resisting just as well. I spent that summer in a state of sexual excitement and anxiety.

A few weeks before the end of the summer, a new face appeared at the camp. It was not clear where Danny Gordon had come from or why he was there. He was, however, the best looking person any of us had ever seen. He had a body like a Greek God, with dark hair and an infectious smile. He wore his good looks and charisma easily and in a perfectly natural way. He had sex with almost all the female staffers, including my girlfriend, but it was impossible to feel any jealousy. He never boasted or even spoke of it. It was just a phenomenon of nature, to be accepted for what it was.

When summer came to an end, I returned for my last semester of high school. I had scored over 1,400 on the SAT tests and had a grade point average of over 4.0 (we got an extra point for honors classes). I had also scored high on the ACT test that determined eligibility for the National Merit Scholarship awards. Scholarship offers addressed to me began to pour into my high school. We had no college councilor, and I did not know any adults who could help me choose a school. My brother was graduating from the University of Chicago and I had spent time down there. The U of C was considered to be of Ivy League stature—except that it was in Chicago. The school also offered an "early decision" option: if one agreed to go if accepted, they would make an early decision on your application. Doing this meant that I would not have to look at and fill out applications for other schools, which was also appealing. I spoke with my parents and told them that I would only do this if I could live on campus. It would be as if I were away at school, except I would be on the South Side of Chicago. They were in awe of the University and were very happy with this arrangement. It also depended, of course, on getting a scholarship as well as being accepted. Tuition was $1,500 per year at that time. By the middle of October the answer had arrived. I would enter the University of Chicago in October 1962.

The last semester flew by. I still had my work permit, even though I had been fired from the commissary job, so I got out of school early. I had a really good English teacher. Mr. Skolnik had a great sense of humor and was much more engaged with the students than the rest of the faculty. One of the requirements in twelfth-grade English was around poetry. We were told to pick a poet, prepare a report, and read some of their poems aloud. I picked Alan Ginsberg as my poet, and decided to read "America" from his *Howl* collection. "America" was not only a rant against the government and consumerist values, it also used the "F" word over and over again. "Fuck you, America, with your Atom Bomb" was a representative line.

You could get thrown out of school for saying "Fuck." But could you get thrown out if it was part of an assignment? And would they really throw out the student who was accepted to the best school of any graduate? It was a wonderful moment for me. I am not sure how good it was for Mr. Skolnik, but he certainly did nothing to stop the performance. And he retired soon afterward.

Music continued to be an important part of my life. I loved to sing. I was allowed to join the Boys' Chorus, but was told to stand in the back and mouth the words. I just couldn't seem to carry a tune and didn't know how to learn. Most of my singing was in the shower or while walking home from school. All of it was a cappella.

My mother had left the Zionist Organization and taken a job working for Albert Grossman, the owner of a Chicago nightclub called The Gate of Horn, who also produced musical events in town. His sister, Devera, was a close friend of my mom's and introduced them. My mom was a great secretary and Al needed someone to work in his office several days a week. He wanted to pay her "under the table" in cash, which was fine with her. She met all of the folk music personalities who came into the office and even became friendly enough with Odetta, the legendary folk singer, to be invited to her wedding. I got a ride from Odetta and her husband when they were going to New York the same time I was. The ride included a free concert on the way.

When Albert left for New York to create Peter Paul and Mary and manage Bob Dylan, he owed my mom several months back pay. He never sent her the money. My father was incensed and wanted to call him out and let Devera and her husband know what had happened. My mother forbade it. She knew Devera idolized her older brother and did not want to interfere with that relationship. They remained friends for the rest of their lives, and my mother never said a word.

After Al left, his partner Frank Freid took over the booking business and my mom continued to work for him. I would go around to stores putting up concert posters for some extra cash. Frank was also responsible for my moment of celebrity and popularity at Lake View High.

Frank had booked Johnny Mathis for eight shows at the Shrine Auditorium in downtown Chicago. Johnny was at the height of his popularity. "Chances Are" and "The Twelfth of Never" were *the* make-out songs of the day. It was sure to be a great success. Frank asked if I wanted to organize the ushering crews for the shows. I would get paid and everyone else would be volunteers and get in free. Suddenly, I was the most powerful person in my high school. Of course I recruited my friends, but that still left so many spots open. People who had never spoken to me were suddenly crowding around my table at lunch begging for a shift. I thoroughly enjoyed my moment in the sun.

The concerts themselves were a zoo. White teenage girls were fainting in the aisles and crying, "Johnny, I want to have your baby." I was sixteen years old and the only homosexual I knew was the bus boy at the local deli who called himself Tinkerbell, but even I could see that Johnny would be more interested in me than in them. It didn't seem to make any difference. We did meet a group of girls who had come to one of the shows from South Shore, at that time still one of the few White neighborhoods left on the South Side. They asked what club we belonged to—perhaps we could arrange a "mixer" with both of our groups? I invented The El Dorados on the spot and got the phone number of the club president. A date was set for this North Side/South Side party.

On the night of the party a few of my friends and I arrived early. We decided to leave and see if we could find some booze to bring back. This meant finding a liquor store with someone hanging out in front who would be willing to go in and buy a few bottles for us in return for some cash. By the time we returned to the party, the police had arrived and there was a full scale riot going on. Some South Side boys had decided to protect their turf (and their women) from the invaders, and someone had called the cops. We left the scene without ever going back inside the house, went back to the North Side and got drunk on the booze we had bought for the mixer.

A few years later, Frank produced The Beatles concert at Comiskey Park, home of the Chicago White Sox baseball team. He gave me two tickets. The place was packed and I quite literally did not hear a single note of music during the whole two hours of performance. Quite a contrast to the folk concerts I was used to attending.

I also had my first girlfriend from Lake View. Shirley was a semester behind me, which meant that she was about a year older than I was. She was an outsider—half Jewish and half Christian. She hung with the Hoods. Her boyfriend rode a motorcycle and had either left town or was in jail, depending on whom you asked. All I knew was that he wasn't around, and Shirley made it clear that she wanted to spend time with me. Mostly we made out. She had her limits, but never spelled them out and liked to keep me guessing and trying. I was happy to play that game as well. Ultimately Ricky came back and Shirley returned to him. Over the next several years we would continue to repeat this pattern on an occasional basis. It was Shirley that I took to hear The Beatles, but even that was not enough to get me to the next level.

Virginity hung heavy over me—as it did over most of my classmates. There was a final assembly on the night before graduation. Afterward I found myself with a couple of classmates who were not close friends, but who I liked well enough. We decided that we were not going to graduate as virgins and drove down to the near South Side, where one of the guys was sure we could find a prostitute to help us with our problem.

This was January in Chicago—cold and windy. We were three white teenagers driving around a black neighborhood looking for a prostitute. Someone directed us to an small apartment building. There was a woman looking out of the first floor window and she waved to us. We went in one at a time to do the deed. It was dark and dingy and the woman seemed as old as my mother. She slipped a condom on and guided me through the process. It took about fifteen minutes for all three of us.

We started back toward home, riding in silence. Within a few blocks we were pulled over by the police. They asked what we were doing there. I said "we got lost" and the cop said, "No, you got laid." He made it clear that we needed to give him some money or else he would pull us in and call our folks. We gave him the rest of our cash and made our way back to the North Side.

When I got home, everyone was asleep. I went into the shower, turned the water on as hot as I could stand it and scrubbed my crotch while saying to myself "that wasn't sex, it wasn't sex, it wasn't sex."

The next day we graduated high school. I was voted "Most likely to Succeed" in my class.

THE LADY ON THE BUS

There were eight months between High School Graduation and college orientation in the Fall of 1962. I needed
to find work.

My parents had a close friend whose daughter, Joan, had
married a young rabbi. Joan and Irv, her husband, had two
children, one of whom needed medical attention. Irv decided
he needed to go into business and make real money instead
of being a clergyman. He pursued a doctorate in psychology
even as he cofounded a market research company with offices
on North Michigan Ave. He could use me as an office boy.

During High School I had occasionally worked for Irv's
company, Creative Research Associates, doing mall intercept
studies. I hated doing it, but the money was good. Now I
could move into the office, which had to be much more interesting than any other job I could get—which was bound to
be manual labor. I had been helping my father on his truck
for years, and I understood manual labor first hand. I was
happy to join the office staff. All the employees were young.
The secretaries amazed me. They were by far the sexiest adult
women I had ever been near—all dressed up in nylons and
heels and looking so good.

There was a lot of work and I put in overtime every week.
Some of it was boring, but part of my job was to move both

of my bosses' cars every hour or so, as they parked below the building in underground Chicago where parking was "one hour only" and hard to come by. I could race their cars around the tunnels several times a day—we believed that radar guns could not work on Lower Wacker Drive. Once I was sent to a town in Wisconsin, about seventy-five miles from Chicago. Saul, Irv's partner, handed me his keys and said, "You do know how to drive a stick, don't you?"

I really wanted to drive to Wisconsin. Hell, I wanted to drive anywhere. So I said, "yes," thinking, how hard could it be? The car broke down about thirty-five miles up the interstate. I had been driving in second gear all the way, which accounted for the terrible sound the engine was making. I pleaded ignorance of the problem's origin and I think Saul wanted a new car anyways because he didn't get angry with me at all.

In the spring and summer of that same year, the Civil Rights Movement reached Chicago. Chicago was probably the most racially segregated city in the country. Black people were not seen on the North Side after dark, unless they worked there (usually as busboys or dishwashers, never as waiters or waitresses). There were lots of pissed-off people on all sides, and tempers flared.

I joined the Congress on Racial Equality, better known as CORE. I was one of a handful of whites, including an Irish guy whom people called Priest—which he was not. I knew why I, as a Jew, understood racism, but why him as an Irishman? "Are you kidding? We're the Niggers of Europe" was his reply to my inquiry.

I was just seventeen and white, and there wasn't that much for me to do aside from helping out around the office and joining an occasional picket line. It did bring me to some places I might never have experienced. Like sitting on a curb late one night drinking very cheap wine with gang kids on the near West Side. Another was going to what were called "Zebra Parties," for obvious reasons. It was there I first heard "Monkey Time" and saw people dance in a way I had never seen before. They were dancing together, but usually not touching, and moving their bodies in such a free and beautiful way. It was my introduction to the Blues.

The other highlight of this period was meeting Dick Gregory. Dick was a headlining comedian—A black man doing very well in what was certainly a white man's world and who was putting everything at risk by using his position to speak truth to power. Dick ultimately became a great advocate for healthy living, but at the time smoking heavily was part of his comic persona as well as a bad habit. I was at a CORE Benefit and when Dick appeared on stage he asked if anyone had a cigarette for him. I ran up and offered my pack. He said "Hey, my first white cigarette." My meeting with Dick Gregory.

I couldn't wear my CORE button at work, but I put it on as soon as I left the office. I rode the Addison St Express Bus home. Often I would stay late, but when I left on time I would sometimes run into my mother, who took the same bus. On one particular day that summer of 1962, my mom was sitting in the back of the bus with a woman she knew from work. She introduced me to her and the woman asked "What does that button mean—CORE?" "That's Congress On Racial Equality," I answered. She then turned to my mother and said: "Don't worry-he'll grow out of it."

My mother just looked at me. She knew what was coming. I stared at the women and said, in a voice that could be heard all through the crowded bus, "If I'm going to grow up to be like you, I'd rather drop dead right now." I have thought about that lady many times over the years, and have come to be grateful to her for helping me stay true to myself and my intentions.

The organizers of CORE and other civil rights groups quickly came to realize that the white people who joined them wanted to help, but still carried an assumption that they knew better than black people what black people should do. As a 17-year-old kid I didn't tell anyone anything at CORE, but I understood when they told us to go back to the White Community and organize against racism there.

So, I didn't have much to do that year. I hung out at Dave Fishman's house on the weekends. His parents had a summer cottage they went to for long periods of time, so we had a house and a car to use. We didn't do much, but at least there were no adults telling us what to do. During the week I would take long walks in the evening with my friend Sheldon. We would sit on the statue of General Sheridan at the corner of Belmont and Sheridan/Lake Shore Dr. I would smoke cigarettes. Since I had a job I no longer had to steal them one or two at a time out of my father's pack. One evening as I was lighting up in front of old Sheridan, my parents drove by. My father leaned out and said "I see you," but nothing happened. The most important thing was discovering Bob Dylan, and learning all the words to all the songs he sang—something I continued doing for many years.

The Unitarian Church opened a coffee house in our neighborhood. We began going there once every week or so.

Sometimes there was a folk singer and other times there were discussions on different topics—usually current events. One evening the question of Universal Community Service was put up for consideration. All males had to register for the draft when we turned eighteen. The War in Vietnam had not begun and there was not an active draft. I knew that people had been drafted during World War II and Korea (Elvis Presley being drafted in 1958 was one of the big stories of that year), but after Korea it was pretty inactive. Still, the question of one's debt to society and service to one's fellow citizens in some form was a topic of interest—especially to young men.

We went around the room giving our opinions about the topic. As an active debater and general know-it-all, I had an opinion about everything. Still, when it came my turn, all the arguments on every side of the issue came flying into my head. I just didn't know and couldn't even speak. It was a shattering experience. I felt like my whole inner self had crumbled. I was left with an unease I had never experienced before. It was a feeling that lived with me all through my college years and did not begin to be resolved until I faced the question of the draft and my relationship to it in a real and consequential way several years later.

Over the Labor Day Weekend I had use of my parents' old Ford. Dave and I decided to drive down to St. Louis to see the Cubs and the Cardinals play their traditional Labor Day double header. On the way down, just south of Springfield, the car threw a rod. It was finished. I had to call my folks and tell them where I was, what had happened, and that the car wasn't coming back. My father said that I shouldn't either, but we hitched back to Chicago and by the time I got home he had cooled off considerably. A few weeks later, after school had started, my parents showed up at the dorm driving a brand new Pontiac Le Mans Coupe. It was the fastest car I had ever driven, and the radio had a reverb feature that created something of an echo chamber. I remember laying on the car and kissing the hood.

My parents had also moved from our old apartment on Addison St to a smaller place at 3750 Lake Shore Drive. This was a very large, middle class apartment complex. They really couldn't afford the rent, but after my father's first heart attack he was told to move from our third-floor walkup. A cousin was part of the ownership/managing group at 3750, and he arranged for a reduced rent. When the building went condo years later, my parents debated whether to move or buy. This was the first building in Chicago to convert, and no one really knew what would happen. In the end, they decided to buy. The first day of public sales the lines were several blocks long with people wanting to purchase an apartment. It was the only good investment they ever made, and my mother lived there until she died almost forty years later.

Now I was at the University of Chicago, the great Liberal school where being "working class" was a badge of honor among classmates who came from elite prep schools on the East Coast. I had a Lake Shore Drive address and use of my parent's brand new car. There was no way I could convince anyone that I was just a working class kid. Sometimes, timing is everything.

THE GREAT FOOTBALL RIOT

By the time college started, I was ready to party and finally be on my own. I spent orientation week drunk. I remember being passed out on the hood of a car in front of a building. The whole freshman class walked by and saw a body lying there. That would be me.

I was housed in Pierce Tower. It was the year the dorm opened and we were the first residents. I was on the eighth floor in Thompson House, in the boy's section of the dorm. My first roommate, Jerry, was a very compact young man dressed in suit and tie, with a crew cut. He had been on the wrestling team of his prep school. I met him at a dinner with his parents when they dropped him off. His father was an industrialist in Canada. They were very wealthy, and also Jewish. Within a day of their departure Jerry had thrown away all his expensive clothing, stopped shaving and started becoming Jerry. He was the most outrageous person in any group, willing to try anything and with a dead-on sense of the absurdity unfolding before us.

Beyond the opportunity to live away from my home, I really wasn't sure of what I was doing there. It was great to be on my own, except I was living in a dorm room and school would soon begin. And if I hadn't thought of it before, it did not take long to realize that the other students were way ahead of me in their schooling. With all my honors classes and grade point, I did not "pass out" of any freshman requirements. Most of my fellow students had come from elite private schools or parochial high schools. There was a good smattering of smart kids from Chicago, but the out-of-towners were much more elite.

The University of Chicago presented itself at that time as a great liberal arts school. It was supposed to "teach you how to think" within whatever profession one entered. As a budding lawyer, this seemed perfect for me. What I hadn't realized was that the core curriculum, which everyone took for their first two years, would force me to take classes I did not want to take, and work hard to get mediocre grades at them. I hated the school part of school. I liked staying up all night playing bridge (a passion among my peers) or hearts or poker in the lounge. There were also the Tuesday night "Twist Parties" that the University sponsored. It had live music—very good. It sounded like a Black South Side band. It wasn't until the third time I went that I realized the band was mostly young white guys. It was the Butterfield Blues Band, which featured two U of C students—Paul Butterfield and Elvin Bishop. Paul had traded a flute for a harmonica and had a great gravelly singing voice. Elvin played a mean blues guitar and the other guitar player was the (soon to be) legendary Michael Bloomfield.

Paul was also one of the best pool players I ever saw. I hung around in the Reynolds Club—a somewhat disreputable lounge area with several old pool tables, which offered a variety of table rolls and other idiosyncratic challenges to one's skills. I hung with a group of mediocre players who liked to gamble for small amounts but stayed away from anyone who could really play.

During that first year I also worked many weekends at CRA. This was in the per-historic era, when documents had to be typed, proofread and corrected on stencils, get printed and then collated by hand. At CRA, everything was a rush. Irv was gulping ulcer pills and his partner Saul was an Israeli psychologist who drank copious cups of coffee and was constantly producing work during production so that there was always a looming deadline. Hence, lots of work on weekends for me and whatever friends wanted to pick up extra cash. At the end of the year, their office manager quit and they asked me to work as manager during the summer and train my replacement. But that is another story.

In the meantime, life in the dorm was something of a disaster. The head of the house was a friend of my brother's who was in grad school in Psych with him. He and his wife were very likable—or so it seemed to me. Living with them turned out to be something else. Joanne was wonderful and we were all in love with her. Arnie was a prick. One day at breakfast we noticed the absence of one of our dorm mates was was from the farming Midwest and never missed breakfast. Arnie said that he had left school in the middle of the night without saying anything to anyone. He was ashamed of his failure and Arnie made a few jokes aimed at him. I called him out on it. He told me to shut my mouth. He was in charge and he could say whatever he wanted to. I just held my breathe and my tongue—for a change—and never spoke to him again. Late in the year, while they were away for a long weekend, a group of guys put a hose under the door of their suite and flooded it. They were sorry for Joanne, but they were doing it anyway. I had no part in the gesture, but I certainly appreciated the sentiment. Arnie got his revenge on me anyway. Because of my age, the university required a letter from the head of the dorm house as to my readiness to live independently in an apartment during my second year. He said I was not ready to be that responsible, and I had to spend my second year in a University housing building that had apartments but restrictions like a dorm. A prick to the end.

I ended the year with about a C+ average. When the scholarship letter came from the University, my grant was reduced by a few hundred dollars. My parents attributed this to neglecting my studies, which I certainly had done. This happened the second year as well. Spring Quarter I got an A, a B, a C and a D—expressing exactly my interest in the subject matter. It happened my third year as well, when I was on the Dean's List (a good thing) for my grades. The University simply cut grants every year because they knew we would somehow come up with the money and there would be more to attract incoming freshman.

That summer after my Freshman year at CRA was very interesting. I was there as an "adult," as the Office Manager, and not the Office Boy. The secretaries did not work for me, but I no longer worked for them. I worked with them to make sure that the documents got produced. I was is charge of the part time office staff, which could be up to 10 or 15 people depending on the number of projects at the time and their size. I also hired this staff. That entailed some important decisions.

The year before, I had worked with the part timers in whatever work was going on. I was attracted to two girls who worked at CRA that year and were likely to call again for a job. I knew that I didn't want both of them there at the same time. That would only confuse me and I would end up with neither. I needed to decide beforehand. I opted for the daughter of one of the interviewers, who were typically "housewives" looking for part time work. Her name was Judy. She lived in Skokie. She became my girlfriend and ultimately my fiancee, and she certainly figures in this and other stories.

I also hired my friends. Burton was one of my two close friends at Lake View. He was smart but very shy around girls. He had spent much of high school ducking under the windows in his room that faced the apartment of the girl across the alley. She was a year or so older than us and very buxom. We were convinced that she knew Burt was peeping, and put on enough of a show to keep him coming back, without ever revealing more than a little.

Burton fell in love with pretty much every girl he met. He would vow to us that he was going to ask whoever she was out "soon," but soon became later and then never. If one didn't date a girl that Burt liked, one would never date a girl. So, when Burt expressed his admiration for Judy and intention to ask her out, it did not deter me from asking her myself. We dated that summer and in the Fall she went off to enter The University of Illinois at Champlain-Urbana. Burt would be returning there for his second year. Early that first semester, Burt actually asked her out and she accepted. They dated that year at school. It wasn't exclusive—Judy also dated the film columnist from the school newspaper. His name was Roger Ebert. Still, I saw Judy during every break and vacation, and she came up to go to "Junior Prom" with me. She wore a very sexy, low cut gown and afterward we went back to my dorm/apartment. The rule was that visitors of the opposite sex had to be signed out at 1:00am. We straggled down at about 3 am.—with the staff sitting around the lobby wondering when this last guest would emerge from the elevator. Everyone just laughed at our appearance and we walked out. That summer we worked at CRA again (the person I had trained had left) but Burton did not. He never spoke to me again. I was saddened. I certainly never would have asked Judy out if Burt already had, but I didn't feel guilty about courting her. But there was nothing I could do— we just couldn't be friends anymore.

During my second year of school I was more unhappy than as a freshman. Classes were even harder, and even less interesting. I was advised by my councilor that I would be better served taking biology as my science requirement rather than physical science. I took the first test about two weeks after class began. I failed it completely and knew there was no chance for me to pass. So, I stopped doing anything. I didn't waste any time or energy and just took my failing grade. I signed up for the physical science class for non-science majors. I squeaked out a "D" with the help of a physics major from my old dorm who took pity on me and tutored me into a barely passing performance.

There was an incident early in the school year that fundamentally altered my relationship to the University. The U of C had been a "Big Ten" school, competing in all the sports with conference members. For the past several decades they had not been competitive in any of the major sports—especially football. The school had canceled the football program and made a virtue of their decision in terms of bolstering their intellectual credentials. Many of us who attended U of C shared that attitude—it was one of the things that had attracted us. The school had a "football club" that played a few games locally. Now it was proposing joining with other schools to form some kind of league. There was a game scheduled on campus and a bunch of students decided to disrupt it as a protest. It was kind of a serious lark. Students at other schools had held protests—we would have ours.

Before the game started, students started running out on the field, which was the Midway built for the World's Fair of 1893, and which now served as a barrier between the University and the Black neighborhood to the South. There was a lot of yelling back and forth between the pro and anti football contingents and someone grabbed the ball and started throwing it around. The campus police arrived. By this time I was standing and arguing with two ex-Thompson house boys. One had been on the basketball team. The other was his roommate from Freshman year who, after a few beers, would take the basketball player, turn him upside-down and stuff him into a garbage can just for fun. He was also known to climb up the outside of Pierce tower between the 7th and 8th floors, also after a couple of beers.

The campus police came over and assessed the situation. They immediately arrested me for assaulting the basketball player and the giant. They told me to apologize to them and then took me away. Ultimately they let me go with a warning that I was now on their list of troublemakers. Surprise— the school was not on my side. It was just another bullshit institution I would have to navigate through. I really wanted to drop out, but had no idea what I would do. My major experience of a "drop-out"was my brother's friend, Sandy. Sandy was really nice and really smart. He had gotten a scholarship to Brandeis—the only one we knew who went away to a good school. He had left Brandeis and returned to Chicago. Everyone spoke of him in kind of hushed tones, as if he were some kind of invalid. It was very depressing. School was hateful, but it was a world I could navigate if I had to. By then I felt that I was going to become a lawyer and also marry Judy. What would dropping out do to this plan? So, I stayed.

Two months later President Kennedy was assassinated.

BANANAS TASTE LIKE BLOOD

Everyone of a certain age (except George VW Bush) remembers where they were when they heard about the shooting in Dallas. I was at the Reynolds Club playing pool and about to cut another class. Someone came in and told us what had happened. I went to the class, where we sat in stunned silence and waited to see if or when he would die. Over the next several days, we watched Lee Harvey Oswald get shot on national TV by the "patriotic night club owner" Jack Ruby and the whole establishment come together around the scenario that this was the work of one lone psychotic shooter. This shooter happened to have been a Marine who defected to Russia and came home with a Russian bride with no consequences for his actions, who had served on an intelligence gathering base in Japan, but had no connection to the CIA. This was as believable to me as Duck and Cover had been. But by now I knew that the "Grown-ups" weren't always stupid—sometimes they were flat out lying to us. And this was one of those times. It was almost impossible to hear other voices through the din created by the media, but nothing about this felt right.

Lyndon Johnson was sworn in as President. The torch passed with minimal disruption. Johnson was even more progressive than Kennedy on domestic issues. He was a Southern

Senator who used all his power to facilitate Civil Rights for black people, and as a Southerner was in a better position to do this than a Yankee from Massachusetts. He was also a consummate politician who knew where all the bodies were buried on Capital Hill. He did not hesitate to use the power he had accumulated in the Senate in the service of his presidential goals. His domestic agenda was great, but on foreign policy he was much more willing to listen to and work with the military—unlike Kennedy, who had learned from the Bay of Pigs and the Cuban Missile Crisis that large elements of the Military and the industries surrounding it—the "Military Industrial Complex" that President Eisenhower had warned about in his Farewell Address—were eager and willing to send the United States into wars all over the world.

In 1964 Johnson ran for his own term as President. He was the "Peace Candidate," who promised that "American boys will not be sent to do what Asian boys should be doing for themselves." He won a landslide victory over Barry Goldwater, the conservative senator from Arizona who had said that "extremism in the defense of liberty is no vice..." He won because people did not want another war. Six months later we we in Vietnam. The War was on.

One other important thing happened that Spring of 1964. The Living Theater came to Campus.

The Living Theater was an avant-garde, political theater troupe founded by Alfred and Judith Mellina. They combined great acting chops with a complete disdain for conventional anything. They were the first theater troupe to feature nudity on stage—a concept that "Hair" took from them and made into a hugely commercial enterprise.

The performance began in complete darkness. Suddenly, a person would stand up in the audience and say something. "I can't live without money. I can't travel without a passport." Someone stood up and said *"Bananas taste like blood."* That line went through me like an electric shock. Then the players came from the audience and the performance itself began.

I didn't understand the line. I don't remember much of the performance. But those words, "bananas taste like blood," planted a seed in my being. They formed a crucial link in the evolution of my consciousness about the empire and its effects, and the relationship of our own lives-even down to what we eat—to what happens in the world outside.

THE FRIENDLY STRANGER

In the Fall of 1964 I would finally be able to live off campus. My friend Jordan and I planned to rent an apartment together. Judy would come up and spend weekends. And I would start choosing my own classes. But first was summer.

Judy and I once again worked at CRA. We went to concerts at Ravinia, the summer home of the Chicago Philharmonic and a venue for many popular groups. We saw Bob Dylan there on a night that threatened rain. As always, we had bought lawn tickets. They were less expensive and besides, we were mostly making out on the blanket with the music as background. Dylan, of course, was different.

The covered seats were for season ticket holders who came for the classical concerts. So, there were lots of empty seats under the tent. As soon as Bob launched his first song, "A Hard Rain is Gonna' Fall," the skies opened and a hard rain indeed began falling. There was a rule that people on the lawn couldn't come in under the tent, even if there were empty seats. Bob invited us in and we accepted his invitation. The ushers were helpless and we were dry. It was a great concert.

Jordan and I made plans to spend a week or two on the East Coast before school started. I had hitched to New York a few times and also gotten rides from people at school. I always had a place to stay when I got there. I would get a ride to the Expressway in South Chicago and hold up a sign that said "student to New York." Sometimes I would get picked up by traveling salesmen who would have me drive for a few hours (or more) so that they could nap. My aunt always insisted on paying for a bus ticket back to Chicago. I couldn't argue, since she let me stay at her place and come and go as I pleased.

This time we were getting a drive-away car. Usually you got gas money for the trip and sometimes even a small payment for driving someone's car from Chicago to an East Coast city. One of our friend's parents owned such a service so it was easy to get a car. In this case it was a small cafeteria truck going to Boston. We would be able to drive through New York, stay there for a few days, and then visit New England in September.

We were on the Ohio Turnpike when we spotted a lone hitch-hiker on the side of the road. We stopped. He was unlike anyone we had ever met. He was from California. He had hair down to his waist and was hitching to New York to meet his girlfriend, who was coming in from Europe and together they would hitch back out West. We spoke of this and that and he offered to meet us in Greenwich Village that night and help us get some pot.

I had been hearing about pot all during my second year. Some people I knew had smoked, but I had not been able to get any. I certainly wanted to. All my young life, as a smoker, I had been warned not to take cigarettes from friendly strangers. If there was something in these cigarettes that grown-ups did not want me to have, I wanted it. Now I had my chance. I had met my friendly stranger on the Ohio Turnpike.

That night, Jordan and I got ready to take the subway from Brooklyn into Manhattan. We decided, for some reason I still do not fathom, that we should wear suits and ties on our pot buying expedition to Greenwich Village. I guess we didn't want to stand out. It took everything he had for our friend to assure the dealer that we were OK. We ended up on the steps of St. Mark's Church smoking one of the joints. Jordan kept insisting that we had been cheated, and I just kept getting higher. Eventually Jordan joined me, along with a small black guy who sat with us and smoked our pot, and then invited us to a party in the East Village. We began to walk across town with our new friend. We had taken our suit coats and ties off and looked better for the neighborhood.

As we crossed town, the houses got older and more decrepit. By the time we reached our destination we were in the middle of the old East Village, when it was at its most dismal. We went up the steps of the apartment building and knocked on the door. It opened into a small kitchen. Behind the kitchen was a loft area filled with cots. There were men with needles in their arm lying on every cot. We were in a shooting gallery. The first time I had ever smoked pot, and I was already at the end of the line! I looked at the kitchen, with a large cauldron of what could have been chili, and the junkies in the room behind it. I said to myself "this (pot) is great. This other, not so much." With all the drugs that I did over the next several years, I never put or was tempted to put a needle in my body. When it was offered, I just said "not my thing" and no one ever argued. Hell, it just meant more for them.

The only other detail of that trip that I remember was playing pool in a New England town on a Sunday night. The

Rolling Stones came on the Ed Sullivan Show and sang "Satisfaction." The British Invasion was fully launched.

We got back to Chicago and moved into our apartment. Suddenly, pot was all around. Perhaps it had always been there and I just had not seen it, or perhaps it was new on the scene. Whatever—it was available and I loved it.

Judy was back Downstate at school, but this year I had a place for us to be together. She came up almost every weekend. She was paranoid that someone who knew her family would see us and mention this to her parents, who knew nothing of these weekend trysts. So, even though her parents lived in the northern suburbs and we were in Hyde Park, she rarely wanted to leave the apartment during these weekends. Sex could not take up all of our time, and she felt the need to study. I joined her. I developed the habit of doing papers several weeks in advance, rather than pulling all-nighters on the night before they were due. I would often do them just as quickly, but without the pressure. I put them away and would look at them a few days before they became due. I could make corrections or improvements that way. Also, I realized that if I just went to class during the week I would know what the teacher wanted and could more easily give it to them. These two factors, combined with the fact that I was taking classes of more interest to me (A lot of Russian History and Literature), led to a substantial improvement in my grade point average and put me on the Dean's List that year. My parents did not know that sex and drugs had fueled my academic achievement, but they were very proud of me.

In June, my father had his second heart attack. In those days there were no stints and no by-pass surgery. Everything was open-heart and arteries were cleaned and re-sewn. There was a long period of recovery—if there was recovery at all.

Since I was a young boy I had helped my father on The Truck. I had gone out to the warehouse with him to load and helped him take inventory in the stores, make up the orders, rotate the stock and refill the shelves. He and all the other drivers were "independent contractors." Even though they worked only for Stella D'Oro, they were not treated as employees and had no benefits. This type of arrangement was ultimately ruled illegal by the Federal Government, but it was routine practice in those days. My father was paid strictly on commission, receiving a portion of the sales he generated. If the company ran his route for him (as it would if he went on vacation, for instance) he would earn nothing. We decided that I would run his route that summer so that the family would continue to have an income. I was happy to do so. I also agreed to move back home for senior year. My mother did not drive and it would be easier for everyone if I was there to help. I could stay with friends during the week and come home on weekends. My only proviso was that, as an adult, I expected privacy. My room was to be my room—period. Of course my parents agreed. And, of course, my mother violated this by cleaning my room and finding my stash.

This was 1965. Finding marijuana in their son's drawer was a shock. When they confronted me, my immediate reaction was that they had violated our agreement. It was an invalid search, warrantless and without probable cause, and they had no basis for saying anything about it. I was already practicing law. They asked me to speak with our family doctor. I agreed, partly to placate them and make them feel better, and partly out of curiosity about what he would say. He had been our family doctor for years. He was also a neighbor and had done house calls on a regular basis, and seemed like a pretty good guy. So, I went to his office for a conversation. He did not try to warn me of the dangers of drug addiction (pot=heroin) or even of medical dangers associated with smoking pot, since he did not know of any. He focused on the danger to my parents. He reminded me of my father's heart condition and how my behavior might cause him another heart attack. I pointed out to him that I might decide to drop out of school. Or perhaps I might want to marry someone who was not Jewish. Either of these decisions, according to this logic, might cause my father to have a heart attack. Whose life was I living, I asked him, mine or my parents'? Of course I cared about them. I was willing to do many things to help them, and I did. But I was not going to live my life to make them feel better. My life was my life, period. I went home, told them we had spoken, and we never discussed drugs again.

My father did have two more heart attacks. Neither one was connected to my behavior—which included much that my parents would have rather I did not do. My father was a life-long smoker who ate a typical Jewish-American diet. Every day he experienced multiple changes of temperature. In summer from the heat and humidity of the street and the back of the truck to the air conditioned cold of the store. In winter from the freezing temperatures outside to the overheated inside. He did this between 80-100 times per day. Plus, he didn't handle stress well. He was quietly angry inside almost all the time. He and my mother did not really get along. They were both nice people, but they became worse and worse as a couple. It was a wonder that he lasted until 1978. At age 66 his fourth heart attack killed him. He was in the truck when he felt it. He drove himself home, parked in the lot where he kept the truck overnight, got into his car and drove himself to the hospital. He died that night.

But, meanwhile, it was 1965 in Chicago. I was back living at my parents' house, and Judy was living at hers. She had come back to complete her studies at the newly opened Chicago campus of the University of Illinois. Suddenly, we had no place to have sex on a regular basis. In addition, she did not share my growing interest in marijuana and the culture (or "counter-culture") growing around it. Then her parents discovered that one of the times we were supposedly studying together at the Northwestern University Library (our recurring cover story), the library had been closed. I had been urging her to tell her parents that we were adults and could sleep together if we wanted to. She said that this was "immature." The mature thing to do was to continue to deceive them. Now we had been found out. Her family demanded to know my intentions. I had always wanted to marry Judy and expected to do so. Her father wanted me to ask for her hand in marriage. I met with him and told him I would not ask his permission, since I intended to marry his daughter with or with or without his blessing. He accepted this and I bought an engagement ring.

In the Fall of 1965 I took the LSAT's (the law school admission test). It was my first big exam since high school. It was the hardest multiple choice test I had ever encountered, and I came out convinced that my chances at a top-tier law school were gone. When I got the results, I was flabbergasted. I had done great. I also learned that law schools were only interested in grades from the 3rd year of college. They recognized that students came from many different environments and schools and that the third year was when things evened out and grades achieved then were most indicative of true ability. Dean's List and high LSAT's—I was on my way to the top! I immediately applied to Yale. My future awaited me.

SITTING IN LIMBO

The years 1965 to '66 was also a watershed year in the expanding war in Southeast Asia. The draft had been ramped up and people my age were faced with the reality of having to go into the army. The government was fine with giving students a deferment, but now they were asking schools to turn over the grades of their students, with an eye toward pulling the deferments of those not doing well. Needless to say, the students were not happy. Many were genuinely concerned with academic freedom and the University becoming an agent of the government. Most were concerned with their own safety and keeping their deferment.

At the University of Chicago, the students occupied the Administration building. I played no role in the organizing of this protest, but did spend some time in the building. Any illusion I had had about the University and its role had been left on the football field, and I had no doubt that the University would do whatever it felt was in its own best interests. I knew that the war was wrong, but as a senior with an extended deferment via law school, this was not my fight. It was, however, another good reason to continue my education after college.

Senior year rolled along. Judy and I struggled through our diverging lifestyles—most specifically, my increasing pot smoking and her refusal to even try the weed. We also struggled to find places where we could be alone together. One afternoon we went back to my parents' house while they were still at work. We were in my bed when the bedroom door opened. My father had come home early and needed to put something away in the closet. He quickly realized what was happening and left, closing the door behind him. Judy was mortified. She started crying and said she could never look at my father again. She asked me to take her home. I got dressed and went out to tell my dad I was driving her back to Skokie. He was sitting in the living room, reading the newspaper. His reply was "why isn't she staying for dinner? The traffic will be murder now."

Compounding all this was the fact that I would be in New Haven in the Fall, and she would still be in Chicago finishing up her degree. I did not see how we could continue the way we were going. I remembered an evening a few years back. We had gone to the movies with Dave Fishman and his girlfriend. We saw "The Pawnbroker." I knew nothing about it beforehand. It was playing at the Esquire, one of the few Art Theaters in Chicago, so we figured it must be good. It was the most powerful film I had ever seen. Rod Steiger's performance as a Holocaust survivor whose bitterness destroys himself and all around him touched me so deeply that, after the film was over, I could not move. Finally, as the theater emptied out, my friends half carried me out into the street. That night, as we held each other and talked about the future, Judy looked at me and said "I don't think we will ever get married." I burst out crying—something I had not done since I was a young child. Now, two years later, I realized she was right. Still, I could not bring myself to call it off. I loved her, and it was hard to see a future without her.

When classes ended, my classmates and I had two weeks before graduation. One of the guys in our group knew someone with a house on Martha's Vineyard that we could stay at for a week. I could stop in New Haven on the way and find a place to live for the next school year. Off we went. I found a place a few blocks from the University and even a roommate for the Fall. Then we went to the Vineyard. I had never been there. In fact, I had never been to a truly natural setting before. Growing up in Brooklyn and then Chicago, I had rarely been out of an urban area. A few family or company picnics in the Forest Preserves west of Chicago and a trip around Lake Michigan when I was twelve was about it. Now I was on an Island in the Atlantic Ocean. It was a powerful vista, made much more powerful by the fact that I dropped Acid for the first time. I was on the side of a cliff when the fog began to roll in, and the clay of the cliff dissolved before my eyes. I somehow made it up to the top and came back to the house, where I watched raindrops roll down windows for an eternity. The wonder of the world and the infinite possibilities of existence opened up. It was clear to me that my old life was over, and a new one about to begin.

We returned to Chicago. I went to see Judy and told her it was over between us. She was upset, but not surprised. It was clear that we had been moving in opposite directions for a long time, and that I was not turning around. On the day of graduation, some of the students wanted to wear black armbands to demonstrate their disapproval of the War in Vietnam and the University's complicity in it. Others felt this would detract from the ceremony and that this was "not the place" for such a statement. In the end, some of us wore the bands and others didn't. I did. As we marched down the center aisle of Rockefeller Chapel, I felt the weight of the past heavy on my shoulders. I had done all that was expected of me. I had done it more or less on my own terms. I had graduated from the University of Chicago—though I had more friends among those who lived off the University and its students than among the students themselves. I had been accepted to one of the top law schools in the country— though I had signed whatever petitions I wanted to sign and joined whatever demonstrations I wanted to join. But I hated school, and knew I continued to go because I could not figure out what else to do. I knew that I could not continue to live a life divided for much longer. I was going to have to make a choice, and I honestly did not know what that choice would be, or how I would make it.

That summer of 1966 I felt like I was living in Limbo. I was driving my father's truck a few days a week and then for a more extended period when my parents went on vacation. I spent a lot of time with my old friend Sheldon, who had graduated from Northwestern when I graduated from Chicago. He thought he might become a filmmaker, and I helped him make a film. He knew the fringe crowd at Northwestern, and introduced me to lots of girls. People asked me what I was going to be doing in the Fall. I told them that I would be at Yale Law School—if I went. Everyone laughed— including myself.

The summer was coming to an end and I had to leave. Some of my college friends had spent the summer in Europe. They had bummed around—even living for a while in caves on a Greek Island. At the end they had gone to Morocco and were coming back to the States with bags of Hashish from North Africa. I arrived in New York in time to meet them at the airport. You could watch the incoming passengers from above as they went through customs. It was all I could do to not break out into a cheer when I saw them waved through without inspection. We spent the next couple of days celebrating. Then I was off to New Haven.

One of our friends, Steve, came from New Haven. We had met during orientation week and had been friends ever since. Steve was a strange cat. He came from a working class Catholic family. He hated the Church with a deep and abiding hatred, and never ran out of scatological jokes featuring the Pope, the Priests and the Nuns. I thought this was because of his Catholic School education. There was a joke I knew about a Jewish kid who kept getting thrown out of schools. His parents finally sent him to the Nuns, where his behavior changed radically. At the end of the year, his parents asked him what had happened. He replied that he had seen this guy hanging on a cross in every room, and figured that he was there as a warning to those who might misbehave. It wasn't until years later, when the sordid story of sexual abuse surfaced, with the New England area as a center of activity, that I realized Steve's hatred came from a much deeper place.

Steve and I drove up to New Haven. He stayed with me at my new house. On the morning of registration, we pulled two chairs out in front of the building. Steve pulled out a pipe and some of that great hash from Marrakesh. We smoked and watched the students going to register. All of my years of school flashed before my mind. From Duck and Cover to the great football protest to the incredible boredom of 99% of my classes. How I had stayed in school because I was good at it and there didn't seem to be anything else to do. And the draft. The big bad draft that hung over the head of our whole generation. There was the money too. It would be hard not to be rich with a degree from Yale law. On the other side—who knows? A great big question mark and a big bad world.

We continued to refill the pipe and smoke until I saw my fellow students returning from registration. I turned to Steve and said, "Well, I guess I'm not going to Law School." A couple of days later my parents called. They said that the school had called them asking where I was. I told them I would see them in Chicago in a few days. They were sorry, but I could tell they were not surprised.

ALWAYS CARRY A PURSE

When I got back to Chicago, all I really wanted to do was to go to Europe and do what my friends had done that past summer. The problem, as someone reminded me, was with the draft. Now that I was no longer a student, I could expect to hear from my draft board sooner rather than later. If I was in Europe when that happened, I would either have to cut my trip short or ignore the notice. If I ignored it, I could never come back to The States.

The reality started to set in: I had traded a secure economic future and freedom from the draft for what? I had no idea. I didn't know what I was going to do with my life, and I certainly didn't know how I was going to get out of the army. Part of me was thrilled and excited that I had finally gone my own way. The other part was terrified. Not just about the draft, but because now I was nobody. I was no longer a student, a future lawyer, no longer had a girlfriend/fiancee—no longer knew who I was or if I was anyone. All the identities I had inhabited were gone. Now there was just me, and I had no idea who that was. I was 21 years old, and didn't have a clue.

But first I had to deal with the draft. I had to find another way to get a deferment. I knew that even if I got drafted, I could avoid combat. A degree from the UofC would get me some kind of desk job, or so I told myself. But I didn't want to participate in the war. More importantly, I knew that the Army was run by rednecks, who would destroy a fat little Jew-boy from the big city—these were the only people who had ever hurt me. A gang of hillbillies had pushed me into an alley on Broadway, just a couple of blocks from my house. They hit me, kicked me in the balls and called me a kike. In my mind, all the sergeants and corporals in the army were these guys. I seriously doubted I would survive basic training, let alone the army itself. What the hell was I going to do?

I should say a few words about the draft—that arcane relic of a bygone era. There were several classifications that determined how likely you were to have to serve in the Army for a term of two years. 1A meant you were prime for becoming cannon fodder. "4F" meant they would never be desperate enough to need your service. In between were a number of temporary or provisional classifications. 2S was a student deferment—what I had given up by leaving Yale. There was a work related deferment for those whose jobs were deemed vital to the public interest. Working in a defense plant was one such occupation. So was being a teacher, and there are many teachers retiring now from a profession they grew to love but entered because it got them out of the Army.

In between these was the 1Y—a more or less temporary deferment based on a condition that was not severe enough to warrant a 4F or else temporary in nature. You might get better enough to get killed and were subject to a new physical if the need arose for more bodies.

I did some research. It seemed my only—but still long— shot was to go for a 1Y based upon a psychological condition—lacking the flat feet, trick knee or other physical barrier to service. The best way to do that was to get a letter from a shrink saying that you were too crazy to be in the Army. I reached out to my brother, who was a psychologist, for a recommendation for a therapist. Since he thought I was crazy for not going to Yale, it was not hard to convince him of my sincerity.

The first thing she said when I walked into her office was "If you are here for one of those draft letters, forget it. Find someone else. I don't do that." I spent the rest of the hour convincing her of my sincerity, and began our sessions. I soon figured out that she, like most people my brother's age, was terrified of drugs. They drank, but the mind-altering action of pot, and especially LSD and the other psychedelics, was very frightening for them. This would be my lever.

The notice to report for a physical came. When I asked her for "the letter" she said "I told you I don't write those." I replied that if she did not, my only alternative was to shoot up heroin on the night before the physical, and to go in high. She said I was blackmailing her. I was committing moral extortion, but I pointed out that it was my ass that they wanted to send 10,000 miles away to shoot at people, not hers.

In the end she agreed to give me a letter that said I was seeing her, but not recommending a deferment. I figured this was as good as I was going to get from her and I took it.

A few words about the physical itself. It took place on a typically cold and dreary November day. We were told to report early in the morning to the induction center just west of downtown Chicago. We were told to report at 7:00am, and then had to wait outside the building until the the doors opened at 7:30. There were several hundred young men aged 18-23 in the group, milling around, smoking cigarettes and trying to keep warm. The overwhelming majority were black or brown, with a scattering of lower class white guys. I did run into a fellow I had known in high school and we stood there discussing our strategies for getting out. He planned to disrupt the process whenever possible. I told him of my shrink-related strategy. We wished each other luck as the doors opened. I never saw him again.

We filed into the huge waiting room and began filling out papers with all our personal information, including possible reasons we were not fit to serve. I was already a fan of Phil Ochs, the great protest singer whose "Draft Dodger Rag" listed the various ways you could avoid the draft. I checked all those boxes on the intake document. One of Phil's ways was to say that you "Always carry a purse..." I checked the box that said I was a homosexual. I also gave them the letter from my shrink. Next we were sent into the locker room where we stripped down to our underwear, got into line and were examined by a series of doctors. The highlight was being told to pull down your shorts and bend over while they shined a flashlight up your asshole.

On the way out I was pulled out of line and sent into the office of the staff psychologist. He looked at my letter and my answers on the form. The only answer he was interested in was about my homosexual condition.

I was 21 and hopelessly and unrelentingly heterosexual. I didn't mind gay people at all. It just wasn't me. I had no experience to tell the doctor about. I had not prepared for this moment. So, when he asked me about my homosexuality, I had no idea of what I was going to say. I looked at him straight in the eye and said "I've never done anything, but I think about it all time." He wrote something on my chart and dismissed me. I went back into the locker room, got dressed and joined the rest of the guys waiting to hear their fate.

When my name was called, I was directed into a line. There was a black guy in front of me. When his turn came, the sergeant looked at him and said "Have you ever been in trouble before?" The man said "no." "You are now," replied the sergeant. "You've been found fit to serve your country."

My turn. He looked at my folder and said, "Mister Entin, we hope you get some help with your problem." I got my 1Y—my ticket out.

I was ecstatic. I had fooled the United States Government into thinking I was crazy.

NINETEENTH NERVOUS BREAKDOWN

After the incredible high of getting my deferment there was a quick period of coming down. I was living in a dumpy apartment hotel in Hyde Park. I had no work and little money. I had beaten the draft but still had no idea what I was going to do. I began having terrible pains in my lower back. They would come and go, but when they came, they were very intense. Finally it got so bad that I crawled my way through Hyde Park to The University of Chicago/Billings Hospital and checked myself in.

The first night there was awful. I finally managed to fall asleep, only to be woken up in order to furnish a urine sample. Since I couldn't get out of bed they gave me a bottle to pee into. I somehow managed to do this, but spilled the contents all over the bed. I was immediately identified as a "bed wetter" and treated as unstable.

That day the doctors performed test after test, but found nothing wrong. They decided to do a mylogram on my back. This is like a spinal tap, but more so. I was injected with a contrast dye between the bones of my spine after being strapped onto a table that spun around in every direction. It went on for more than an hour and was the most painful and disorienting experience of my life. I had a few bad Acid trips, but nothing approached the horror of this medical procedure.

When it was over I was wheeled into the hallway outside the exam room and left there on my gurney. I realized that the shifts had changed and that no one knew who I was or where I belonged. I finally yelled long and loud enough to get some attention. When they read my chart and saw that I was an unstable bed wetter they gave me some drugs to calm me down and wheeled me back to my room. That night they did not wake me again for a sample.

In the morning the doctors came to say that the tests had not revealed any problems, and they recommended exploratory back surgery. At that point I checked myself out of the hospital against medical advice. I went to my parents' home and laid on their couch for the next six weeks while trying to figure out what to do next. I did not return to a hospital again until 2013, for outpatient surgery on a torn shoulder from a slip and fall accident.

For the first couple of weeks I just laid on my back hoping the pain would lessen. A friend of a friend of my parents recommended some exercises I could do on the floor. I had never heard of Yoga but later discovered that these exercises were part of a yoga routine. Gradually the pain began to subside, but still hurt for several hours a day.

Friends came to visit. They brought pot for me to smoke, thinking it might help with the pain. Instead, it intensified it to the point that I was literally climbing the walls trying to find a position that would feel comfortable. After what seemed like hours, I finally felt well enough to lie down and I immediately fell asleep. When I woke up my friends had left and my parents were tip-toeing around trying to keep from disturbing my rest.

As I lie on the couch, trying to read and watching a lot of daytime television, I did some thinking about what had happened and my situation going forward. I understood that my back pain, for which no doctor could find a cause, was my way of having what was in those days called a "nervous breakdown." I came to realize that while I had thought I had out-maneuvered the government to get my 1Y, the reality was that they had driven me crazy with anxiety over serving in the army, and that I really had earned my deferment the hard way. My elation and relief turned to ashes in my mouth.

By the time I felt well enough to go out it was late January, 1967. I had been speaking with Judy on the phone during my convalescence. She said her folks would be away for several days and invited me to come up. The city was just digging out of the storm of the century, but I fought my way through the snow down Irving Park to the Sheridan Road El Stop, took the train to Howard St and found a taxi willing to drive into Skokie. I came home fully recovered and ready to at least take a step into the future.

ALMOST BUSTED
(TWICE IN ONE NIGHT)

I considered getting a job. I went to an employment agency, filled out the paperwork and was sent on a few interviews. One was to be an adjuster for an insurance company. When I came back to the office, the employment counselor told me that they were impressed, but they were "a little leery of my long vacation." I said thank you very much and ended my search for a career in the business world.

I took a job as a social worker. As a University of Chicago graduate with a degree in Sociology, this was easy enough to get. I was assigned for my six week training period to a unit on the Black West Side of Chicago. All of our "clients" were women with children, who were receiving Aid to Families with Dependent Children—or AFDC as everyone called it.

In order to qualify for this assistance, it had to been verified that the family unit consisted only of the woman and her child(ren). If there was a man living in the apartment, the family was ineligible. My job as a social worker was to make sure there was no evidence of male occupancy.

I was a twenty-one year old kid supposed to spy on these older women and their children, with the power to make their only source of income disappear. I would go into their apartments, look around and say "you need some new beds for the kids," say goodbye and write up a recommendation for new furniture, a table or something else. I never reported evidence of a man, and no one ever got a new bed or anything else I recommended. At the end of six weeks, when I would be assigned a permanent desk, I quit the agency and went back to the apartment hotel I had moved into after leaving my folks' house. Those six weeks in the field taught me far more than my years at the University about Sociology and how the social order operates.

My classmates had all left Chicago for graduate school or wherever the next chapter of their lives was going to be played out. I still knew a bunch of people who hung at around Hyde Park--the people who

I played cards and pool with, smoking pot and generally hanging out

That night we gathered at Erica's apartment. Erica was Doug's girlfriend. Doug was the central figure in our group. He was handsome, charming, intelligent, witty and fun to be around. He was also brutal, cutting, dark and solitary. He was, although we did not have the name then, a classic bipolar individual. Since meeting Erica he was on a perpetual high, and we often gathered at her apartment on the top floor of the apartment hotel to wait for Doug to come home from his bar-tending gig. A neighbor, seeing all these men coming and going from the apartment, deduced that Erica was a hooker and called the police.

That night we were supposed to score a pound of weed and were waiting for the call to come over and buy it. About ten minutes after Doug, arrived there was a pounding on the door and a voice yelling "police-open the door." Doug grabbed handfuls of pills and was running into the bathroom when the cops broke through the door and burst in. They saw Doug running into the bathroom and ran after him, but he was able to flush most of them before they grabbed him.

The police immediately realized that Erica was not a hooker and that this was not a cat-house. Still, there were drugs visible and they called a squad car to come and pick us up. I was sitting on the bed, stoned out of my mind and just silently watching everything. I had two joints in my cigarette pack, but otherwise I was clean. After about 15 minutes of waiting for the squad car, I asked the cops if I could use the bathroom. They said yes, looked through my pockets and let me go into the John. I took the two joints out and flushed the toilet. It went down real slow—probably because of all the pills—and the joints floated on top after the flush was over. By now the squad car had come and the police yelled for me to come out. I closed the lid and left the bathroom. In the meantime, our connection had called to tell us we could come over.

They took us down to the precinct house and gave us a thorough search. They even opened my pack of cigs. Since there was nothing on my person, they charged me with being "in a disorderly house where drugs were present" and told me to show up in court the next morning. Doug and Erica were charged with possession as well as "keeping a disorderly house."

When we got back home we called our connection and explained the situation. We all agreed that it would be best to do the transaction the following day, but they invited us over for a taste of the goods. We got into my dad's Pontiac and drove over. On the way back to Hyde Park at about 3:00 a.m. we had to decide whether to go straight home or to go downtown to eat at "The Little Corporal," a great all night spot in Downtown Chicago. We pulled into the parking lot near the Museum of Science and Industry to decide, then pulled back onto the Outer Drive to go Downtown and satisfy our munchies. Within a few minutes there were police lights blinking behind us. Rick had a couple of joints left from the sample. I begged him to throw them out the window, but instead he put them into his mouth.

The cops pulled us over. Almost immediately four or five other squad cars showed up. I had never seen so many police in one place. I asked why they needed so many police for a traffic stop and they suggested that if I did not shut up there would be more to come. They said they had observed us pull into and out of the parking lot and suspected us of being part of a burglary ring that was operating in Hyde Park. They demanded that I open the trunk for them. The only thing in it was the spare tire. They also searched us, but they didn't look in Rick's mouth so there was nothing to find. They let us go and we continued into downtown for, by now, breakfast.

Later that morning I went to court. The judge asked a few questions and dismissed the charges against me. Doug and Erica, however, were arraigned on the charges against them. Since the police did not have a warrant, the case ultimately rested on whether they had been "invited" into the apartment or had broken in. If the police told the truth, the case had no chance. However, this being Chicago, the way to ensure the truth was through the execution of well-placed bribes. Erica's father, who lived in California, hired a well connected attorney in Chicago and ultimately the case against them was thrown out.

At this point I realized it would be good for me to get out of Hyde Park and put some distance between myself and that life. I knew people in and around the Butterfield Blues Band. They were going on the road for an extended tour and the bass player, Jerome Arnold, had a place in Old Town that he wanted to sublet for the months he would be away. It was a carriage house a couple of blocks north of North Avenue and just west of Wells St. It was also close to the Yellow and Checker Cab garages. I moved into the place in Early Spring and started my stint as a Chicago Taxi Driver. It was a great way to start my new life.

TAXI DRIVER

I was a born taxi driver. My time riding and driving my father's delivery route had made me familiar with many parts of the city, so I knew where I was going and how to get there in those pre-GPS days. I also understood that time is money, so my naturally aggressive driving style served me well.

Drivers were paid on commission—40% of the fare went to us and the balance to the company. Out of that 40% there were, of course, deductions. I quickly learned the various ways one could scam the company and increase my earnings. The most important of these was to negotiate a flat rate with the customer on a longer trip—giving a discount if the trip was off meter so that the customer paid less, but you kept more of the fare. This meant that your "available light" on the top of the cab stayed on, and a roaming supervisor might see that you had not turned your meter on. In the real world, the odds were very much against this happening and I never knew anyone who got caught doing this.

I also quickly learned how to be a high earning cab driver even within the confines of the "legitimate" aspects of the business. In Chicago, taxis are an integral part of the transportation system. The ever changing and awful weather made "hopping into a cab" an attractive alternative to waiting on a bus or walking short distances. Fifty or more trips in an 8 hour shift was not unusual. The best trips were the short ones that took you to a place where someone else was waiting for a cab that took you back to where you had picked up the first fare. Shuttling around downtown Chicago and the two miles north of the Loop yielded the most income per hour. When I was on my game, I would become part of the flow of the city, with as many as ten fares or more in an hour. Each had a "flag pull" (the initial fare) and each had a tip, so my earnings were maximized.

I signed on as a "part time night shift driver." This meant I could show up any time on any day after 10:00 am and had to get the cab back by 6:00 am the following morning. I could get up whenever I got up, walk (or catch a cab) to the garage, check out a car, go to breakfast and then work the noon rush hour. I could hang out with friends for a few hours in the afternoon and then work the evening rush, take a break and, especially on weekends, work the clubs, bars, movies, and other venues until the final 3:00 a.m. (weekday) or 5:00 am (weekend) bar closings.

The company monitored our performance through one specific statistic—the ratio of paid versus unpaid miles. They were paying for the gas, maintenance and all expenses associated with the vehicle. They needed a certain amount of income for every mile driven in order to make a profit. As long as you performed within that parameter, you would not get fired. Even with my flat rating, I could always meet their standards.

Working nights, many of my customers were in various stages of inebriation. I quickly learned how to deal with drunks, who were either the best or worst of customers. I learned that I had "ethnic fluidity"—my Eastern European "swarthiness" made me look Greek to the Greeks, Italian to the Italians, and so on. I couldn't pass for Irish, but I could sing an Irish tune. Tips were good.

As a taxi driver, one had to join the union. At the time, the teamsters and the longshoremen were locked in a battle over who would represent the drivers. This was big business, with a lot of money at stake, and the competition sometimes led to violence, with a couple of garages bombed at the height of the battle. The longshoremen won this round, and we all signed up. As a part-timer I did not get much benefit, but there was one incident where I was grateful to be a member.

There were two Ambassador hotels on Chicago's near North Side. The Ambassador East and West were both on Goethe street. What I did not know, early in my career, was that Goethe was a one-way street with a quirk—the one way changed direction between the hotels.

Early one foggy evening I was going from one of these hotels to the other with a fare when I found myself head to head with a Chicago Police car. He turned on his flashers and I had to back up to a place I could pull over. He gave me a ticket for driving the wrong way down a one-way street.

I was caught dead to rights. There would not be much I could say in court to beat the ticket. I was advised by another driver (after he stopped laughing) to call the union. They told me to meet the union lawyer 15 minutes before my court time and to bring $20 for the lawyer's fee. I did what I was told. The lawyer said to "just keep your mouth shut and leave this to me." We entered the courtroom. After exchanging pleasantries, my lawyer approached the bench. A short conversation ensued and then my lawyer came back to me and said "case dismissed." After that I learned to always keep a $10 bill behind my drivers license, so that a cop could always settle the case before a ticket was issued, if they so desired. They usually did.

Just as my 6-week stint as a social worker had taught me more about racial politics and the social structure than my 4 years at university, driving a taxi provided a graduate degree in Institutional Racism. There were black cab drivers in Chicago, but there were also companies that would not hire them. There were two companies on the North Side that specialized in telephone orders. Their (unwritten) motto was "you will never see a black driver at your door."

It was almost impossible for a black person to hail a cab in downtown Chicago. Drivers would just ignore them. I did not like to sit at cab stands, preferring to cruise for fares, but I would occasionally join the queue at a downtown hotel for one reason or another. On this particular night I had joined the cab line in front of the Palmer House, a large business hotel in Downtown Chicago. I had worked my way up to 3rd in line when a black women approached the first cab. Although the cab line was in front of the hotel, people in the street could use it. The driver, who was also black, saw the woman reaching for the door handle and pulled away before she could open the door. The second driver followed him. That left me next. I pulled up, leaned over the seat to open the door for the passenger (something I always did) and she got in.

I was a bit baffled. I understood that some drivers were prejudiced against black people. Some were afraid—as if every black passenger was a potential thief or mugger. But this was a middle-aged black woman carrying packages, and the driver himself was black. What was going on here?

The woman gave me her address and I took her home. She lived in the mid-south side area. I had to take surface streets to get there, and when I dropped her off I had to "deadhead" (drive empty) back into downtown to find another customer, as there were no people on the streets hailing cabs. It was, in economic terms, a "bad fare." As a rule, I realized, it did not pay to pick up black people. Even black drivers knew that. They were out there trying to make a living, trying to maximize their income, and being "racist" was the smart thing to do.

Being young and single, I could afford to have principles. I also wasn't afraid of black people and never sent out that vibe. Plus, I didn't want to offend the taxi gods who were certainly responsible for a lot of the luck that I experienced in my work. I vowed to pick up anyone who hailed me regardless of race, creed, color or gender (women were supposedly worse tippers than men). I trusted that it would all work out—if not on that shift, then on the next one. I was never held up or threatened in any way, and the only person who ever stiffed me was a younger white guy who, after a long ride, jumped out of the cab and ran away without paying.

Beyond that, it really bothered me to see people standing in the cold street, trying to get home after a hard day at work, and having taxi after taxi pass them by as if they were not there. I had read Ralph Ellison's *The Invisible Man*, Richard Wright's *Black Boy* and much of James Baldwin. Driving the streets of Chicago in my cab made their work much more real to me. I did not want to contribute to the physical discomfort and humiliation suffered on a daily basis by these people.

Still, being a cab driver was great fun for me personally. I was good at my job, and realized I could always make a living this way and never have a boss or work for a corporation. I had a car that cost me nothing and every day could bring a new adventure.

Some of the people I had met through driving came from the Albany Park area of Chicago, on the Northwest Side. Like Rodgers Park, it was a Jewish neighborhood, but older and more working class. A few of these people mentioned a friend named "Lou" who still had a place in the old neighborhood. He sounded like an interesting person so I called him one day and went over to visit and get high together.

Lou was of medium height, slender but strong looking. He had thinning hair and a big mustache. He also had a twinkle in his eye and a good, sarcastic sense of humor. We hit it off immediately and began hanging out together. When it came time for me to move out of Jerome's place, Lou decided he wanted to move from Albany Park to the near north side and we looked for a place we could share. We found one and moved in early September of 1967.

PISSING ON THE PENTAGON

By October, 1967, my life had settled into a pretty stable routine. The apartment Lou and I found was in the Diversey/Broadway area of the North Side of Chicago. It was a street-level place below a house. Our landlord was an older man who took our assurances that we were not "hippies," but just a couple of working-class guys.

I was still driving a taxi, as was Lou, but we soon developed a great side business selling small quantities of grass. I had many contacts for scoring decent weed at good prices, and Lou had a wide network of "straight" (in those days that meant non-hippie) people anxious to try out this new high. We could purchase a pound or a kilo (how the metric system came to America), clean it and sell it by the nickle bag—$5 for a shot glass full. The margins were very good. Even if someone wanted five or ten bags, they were still $5 each, with no discount for bulk purchases. I felt a little guilty about this until the night I delivered 20 bags to a friend of a friend. When he opened the door there was a party going in full swing behind him. "Hey, here's the guy with the weed" he yelled, and everyone turned to stare at me. I got the hundred and split as fast as I could.

The cab was a great way to deliver merchandise. The old Checker Cabs had a horn piece that came off, and I could store a small bag or two under the horn without disabling that most critical part of the vehicle. And, as a taxi driver, one simply melded into the urban landscape. One Saturday night, driving into Old Town from the North, I was flagged down. When the man came up to the cab, he pulled out a badge and said "Police." My heart stopped. Then he said, "Turn on your meter," at which point it started to beat again. After a minute, five plainclothes cops piled in and told me to take them the few blocks into the heart of Old Town. When we got there they all quickly piled out again. The one who had hailed me gave me a $10 bill for the $3.50 fare. I knew he expected change, but I just thanked him and he had to run to join his colleagues. It was my best fare of the night.

We would keep the stock in a big glass bowl on the dining room table. If it was inconvenient for us to come and serve a customer, they would just fill up the shot glass we kept next to the bowl and leave the money on the table. It was a very low key and mellow way to make a living. I would just stuff the cash into a drawer in my room and dip into it when the rent or any other bill came due.

A new blues club had opened at the south edge of Old Town, on Wells Ave. It was called "Mother Blues." It was away from the heart of the district, which was a couple of blocks north centered on the intersection of North Ave and Wells St. It was also closer to the black neighborhood that began at Division Street, where the huge and infamous Cabrini–Green housing project was located. The result was that the club became a place where black and white blues lovers could freely mix. Muddy Waters and Howlin' Wolf played there almost every Monday and Tuesday night respectively, when their regular West and South Side clubs were closed. From Wednesday to Sunday it might be Buddy Guy and Junior Wells, James Cotton playing Harmonica or Otis Rush blasting out the cutting edge of Urban Blues. Doug was the service bartender, making drinks for the waitresses to deliver and I had shared some good grass with the doorman. I never had to pay to get in or for a drink. It was blues heaven. I was there every night for at least an hour or two. Taxi drivers were not allowed in bars while on duty (you could go in to announce your presence to a customer who had called a cab) but there was always a line of cabs parked outside of Mother Blues.

I was also seeing Judy for occasional post-breakup sex. She took a trip to Greece and came back smitten with a Greek Revolutionary she had hooked up with over there. I wasn't jealous, but it definitely fueled my imagination. Lou suggested that, if I wanted to be a revolutionary, perhaps I should start here by going to the upcoming March on the Pentagon, taking place on Oct. 17. I agreed. He and I, along with a few other friends, drove to DC. We landed in Georgetown, and within an hour I had found us a place to crash for the night. In the morning we set off to the Lincoln Memorial. From there we would go to the Pentagon, where, according to the Yippee contingent, we would levitate the building and raise everyone's consciousness.

No one knew what would happen. Rumors swirled about an armed response, troops and tanks and trucks deployed to stop us from reaching our objective. In the meantime, a lineup of antiwar speakers orated from in front of Lincoln's chair.

Several of us had ended up at the monument, to the right of where the speakers were speaking. We were passing around a joint when a guy came up and said that the march was starting soon and asked if any of us wanted to be monitors. I said "sure", got up, and waved goodbye to my friends.

I followed him over to where the marchers would be lining up. There were about 20 people standing there. We were told to spread out across the road and link arms. We would be in the front line of the march. Then we were told "Don't stop, 'cause there are 100,000 people behind you." After a few minutes, we were off to the Pentagon.

The distance from the Lincoln Memorial to the Pentagon is about 2 miles. Things fell apart about half way there in terms of any organized presence, but I continued to follow the route to the Pentagon itself. There were three flat-bed media trucks filming the confrontation between Federal Marshals who surrounded the building and the motley crew facing off with them.

I worked my way to the front of the crowd to check out the scene. There were all these kids standing belly to belly with the Marshals. I was so happy to be there among them. It was like standing before the Bastille as the French Revolution began.

The marshals started hitting people with their batons. One was beating on the guy next to me. Without thinking, I grabbed the baton out of his hand. The other guy ran off and I was left standing there holding the stick. For a moment everything felt frozen—like a tableau. Then I quickly threw the baton over the heads of the marshals. The marshal in front of me grabbed my tee shirt and started yelling "get this one." I pushed him in the chest, ducked under the media truck and rolled out the other side. I came around to the back of the crowd. I had a scraped knee—the price of escape.

After a few hours, the crowd began to thin out. It was starting to get dark and cold, after a warm and sunny day. A few hundred of us were left, with nowhere better to go. Food and water miraculously appeared and we settled in. After darkness fell, someone started a bonfire. I threw my draft card in to fan the flames. I heard a guy behind me muttering to himself, saying "I'm tired of all this bullshit—it's time to head for the hills." I went over to him and we talked. He was part of an anarchist collective in New York and we made plans to meet in The City. Finally I fell asleep. I woke up in the middle of the night, cold and desperately needing to pee. I walked over the building, parted some shrubbery and pissed on the Pentagon.

Morning came and we left. I walked to the bus station and got a ticket to New York City, where I had a place to stay with my aunt and her boyfriend. They had spent the weekend driving around with the car lights on, to symbolize their support for the troops and the war they fought. But I was family, so they gave me a place to stay anyway.

I found my friend from the march in his East Village apartment. As soon as I came in, he put "Alice's Restaurant" on the record player. I had never heard it before. I don't think I even knew that Woody had a son, but Arlo felt like he was a Guthrie for a new generation. We talked about what to do next. I said I would come back soon to join the collective. From his place I walked across Lower Manhattan to the Holland Tunnel and started my hitchhike back to Chicago.

PART II

I AIN'T MARCHING ANYMORE

When I got back to Chicago after my adventure at the Pentagon, someone directed me to The Chicago Area Draft Resistance, or CADRE, as they called themselves. A fellow named Jeremy was sitting behind an old, scarred up desk in a nondescript office decorated with posters and signs about resisting the war. I told him about my experience at the Pentagon and throwing my draft card into the bonfire. I wanted to know what I could do to follow up on this and become involved in the antiwar Movement.

Jeremy was a mild looking man, abut my age, wearing kind of old-fashioned eyeglasses. He did not look like a revolutionary at all. He explained to me, in a very nice way, that burning a draft card was essentially a meaningless act. "It could have been a library card," he said. "It's technically illegal but no one has ever been convicted of doing it, because of free speech issues. If you want to make a political statement, you need to get a new card and mail it back to the Government with a note explaining that you are returning the card because of your opposition to the war and expressing your non-cooperation with the draft." At that point," he went on to explain, "they will send you a notice to appear for a new physical. When you don't show up, they will reclassify you 1-A and draft you. When you don't show up for induction into the army, they will arrest you for refusing induction and you will get 2 to 3 years in a Federal prison."

He went on to say that The Resistance, as they called their Movement, saw this as both a personal and political statement. Muhammad Ali had very publicly refused to be conscripted and his actions were an inspiration. For white, middle class students and young people like us, finding ways to avoid the army was much easier than for poor people and, especially, people of color. If we truly opposed the war, if we really believed it was an evil and murderous excursion that was poisoning our own country, even as it was slaughtering the peasant of Vietnam, we had to put ourselves in the path of the machine. We had to stand up and be counted. We had to be brave, if we wanted to be free.

I listened to what he had to say and I told him I would return after the holidays to begin the process. "I'll see you in January," I said. He replied "No you won't—I begin serving my sentence next week." I couldn't believe it—here he was, just days away from entering the Federal Prison in Springfield, MO, and he was still working the desk at the CADRE Office. It gave me shivers then, and it still does today.

My induction into CADRE began with a training in draft counseling, given by the American Friends Service Committee and led by a young lawyer from California named Ken Cloake, who I would meet again when I moved to Los Angeles and would know for the rest of my life. I also began to learn how to speak about the war and our relationship to it, and why we had chosen resistance as our response. We were urged not to try to talk others into doing what we had done. "When the prison door closes, you are serving your sentence alone, and you need to be sure you are willing to do this," was how it was put.

Of course we were young, and there was a certain element of egoism and self righteousness that can accompany this kind of talk and action. Nonetheless, it was clear to me that these were some of the most "saintly" people I had met, and they and their stance resonated deeply with my need to decide for myself what was right and what I needed to do, outside of any authority or traditional teachings.

We often did leafleting in front of the draft centers in Chicago. There was one on the North Side, where I had had my exam, and also one on the South Side. The one on the South Side was near a Catholic boys high school, and the students would come and harass us, call us "Un-American," "pussies" and so on, and threaten us with physical violence. By this time a number of guys had returned from Vietnam ready to speak out, and Chicago was one of the birthplaces for Vietnam Vets Against the War, which today exists as "Vets for Peace." One of these guys was Polish, and had gone to Catholic schools. He came down to the draft center with us a few times to meet the teenagers who were harassing us, and speak to them in their own language. They never bothered us again.

April 3, 1968, was designated as the "Day of Resistance," when we would hold a public rally, collect the cards of everyone who had made the decision to resist, and deliver them to the Federal Building in Chicago. In the meantime, I began traveling around the Midwest with one or another CADRE member, speaking at colleges and churches about the War and why we were resisting it. One of the most memorable of these was an event at a church in a small town in southern

Indiana. When we arrived, we were told that we would be joined by a recently returned vet who had grown up in the Church, and who would present the "other side" of the story.

Southern Indiana is part of the south. The Ku Klux Klan was born there. I looked like a bearded Jewish anarchist. Fortunately, my companion was a seminary student who was more clean cut and Christian looking. As the evening wore on, the vet became more and more agitated, and finally he said "We can win this war. All we need to do is kill every man, woman, child and duck in North and South Vietnam…" We just looked at the congregation and shrugged our shoulders. There was nothing more to say. The sheriff followed our car out of town to make sure we were not ambushed, and we returned to the relative sanity of Chicago.

On April 1st President Lyndon Baines Johnson announced that he would not run for a second term of office. This was considered a major victory for the antiwar Movement, which had taken to chanting "Hey hey, LBJ, how many kids did you kill today" at any public appearance by the President. I was asked if I was still going ahead with my draft decision in light of this development. "Why, is the war over?" was my reply.

April 3rd dawned cold and rainy—Springtime in Chicago. We gathered in front of Roosevelt University on Michigan Avenue. I was the "young" speaker, joined by Benjamin Spock as the adult. Dr. Spock was the author of *Baby and Childcare*, the most influential book on child raising in post-War America. His "permissive" approach was often blamed for the Baby Boomers who refused to do as they were told by their elders. He was one of the first prominent adults to stand with the emerging youth movement challenging the status quo.

When the speeches ended we marched through downtown Chicago to the Federal Building. We were not allowed to enter, but a representative of the Attorney General came outside to meet us and accept the envelope with our draft cards.

The Attorney General to whom we sent our cards was Ramsey Clark. Clark was a staunch liberal and civil libertarian, who had joined the Johnson Administration to further civil rights legislation and found himself prosecuting antiwar activists, including Ben Spock. He stayed with LBJ until he left office in January, 1969, and Clark then joined the antiwar movement. He ultimately became one of the most prominent and outspoken critics of US international policy in the world.

WON'T YOU PLEASE COME TO CHICAGO

The five months between April 3rd and the Democratic National Convention were the most intense of my life.

Our CADRE meetings were like the General Assemblies of the Occupy Movement—they went on forever, everyone had the right to speak and there were police infiltrators determined to create havoc and move people towards violence. It was often obvious who these people were (yelling "off the pigs" in the middle of the meetings was a good clue), but they still made reaching consensus difficult. We did have the calming presence of Professor Staugton and Alice Lynd and a number of members connected with the Quakers to help us keep focused. They reinforced our understanding that using violence to end violence was absurd and self-defeating. We were always looking for ways to get our message out to the larger community, and also to the many young servicemen who came to Chicago from the many military bases in the area.

One of the core CADRE members was a man named Don Tilkie. Don was from Iowa-or perhaps Kansas or Nebraska. In any event, he was a Midwestern school teacher who had experienced a vision of how awful the war in Vietnam was, and how corrupted the society that carried it out had become. All of his patriotism had been turned on its head. He came to

Chicago, let his hair and beard grow out, and became a vocal and vociferous supporter of the North Vietnamese regime— one of the people who would chant "Ho, Ho, Ho Che Mein, the Vietcong are going to win" and carry North Vietnamese flags in demonstrations. He was a gentle soul who took care of the ancient printing press CADRE used to print our leaflets and flyers. But he also, despite the lack of any expertise, decided that he would learn to make bombs and would take out a draft board, when no one was there, with one of his homemade devices.

One night we got a call that a bomb had gone off in his basement apartment. When we arrived at the scene, the police were already there. Don was telling them that the local skin heads must have thrown it through the window, but the neighbors were standing around and I heard one of them matter-of-factly say, "oh, yeah, down there is where they make the bombs." Don was already well-known to the Chicago police. One afternoon when he was walking home, he was attacked by some neighborhood kids who did not like his looks. A police car stopped and the cops got out, assessed the situation and called out "Kick him once for us" before they got back in the car and drove away. The day after the bomb had exploded, Don and his girlfriend left town, never to return again.

On another occasion a school bus came around and gathered folks to go to a wedding at the Indiana dunes, about 1-2 hours outside of Chicago. Everyone was invited— though few of us knew either the bride or the groom. I went with some of the guys who had come back from Vietnam shaken to the core by their experiences and looking for a way to express their revulsion. It was a sunny spring day, we dropped some acid and were "catching a few rays" while observing the scene. The wedding was presided over by a very tall man who came out of the ocean carrying Poseidon's pitchfork. An American flag was being burned as part of the ceremony. The spot where the ceremony was being held was close to the road, and not far from Notre Dame University. A few students were watching from the road, and when they saw the flag-burning, they jumped over the fence and started swinging at those burning the flag. They were completely outnumbered and withdrew quickly, but as we watched the events unfold, it became evident that if we were serious about changing minds and hearts, rooting for the Vietcong and burning flags was not the way to accomplish our ends. We had to find ways to talk with people, rather than at them.

We decided to open a coffee house that would provide a place for the antiwar and military communities to meet. We started looking for a place and found a vacant storefront on Lincoln Avenue, just north of Fullerton Rd. It was just a few doors north of the Biograph Theater, where John Dillinger had been shot down by police in 1934. It was a working class neighborhood, but a head shop had just opened and an "art theater" was also opening across the street. Alice's Restaurant, as we called the Coffeehouse, would be the third "counter-culture" establishment in the neighborhood. We signed a lease and began cleaning and redecorating the room. In this initiative, the women of CADRE took the lead.

One day I was talking to an acquaintance about Alice's and mentioned that it would be great if we could have some music for our opening, which was taking place in a few weeks. He said that he was friends with Terry Collier, a well known African American folksinger in Chicago. He said he would ask Terry if he would play at the event. He agreed, and waived his usual fee. It was a great success and music became an integral part of the scene at Alice's. For a few years the club continued as a focal point for interaction between the young servicemen who came to Chicago on weekend passes and the antiwar community as a whole. Many of the founders of Vietnam Vets Against the War came to Alice's to meet and talk with civilian supporters. After CADRE could no longer keep the place, it continued and became a premier music club in Chicago, and the entire neighborhood became a home to music, theater and comedy clubs to rival Old Town a mile to the South.

Another of our proposed actions was to return to the communities from which we had come, and reconnect to the churches and synagogues in which we had been raised. Since the media always depicted us as "drug-crazed anarchists," talking to these people, who knew us and our families, was a way to cut through this haze and propaganda and present the moral foundation for our actions.

It was in this spirit that I found myself in Rabbi Cohen's study in April, 1968. Not only had Rabbi Cohen officiated at my Bar Mitzvah and Confirmation, he was also a cousin on my mother's side. He was a well known Rabbi in the greater Jewish Community, and his cooperation would be very meaningful for our work. I explained to the Rabbi why I had chosen my path and asked for the opportunity to address the congregation, perhaps at a Friday night service. He refused. When I asked him why, he replied that "he had not yet made up his mind about the War in Vietnam" (after almost five years of fighting). He then asked me how I felt about Israel. Truth to tell, I had no thoughts about Israel. I had grown up collecting money to plant trees in Israel, my mother had worked as a secretary for the Zionist organization and the narrative of *Exodus* (the novel and the film based upon it) were reflective of my own. Still, I looked at Rabbi Cohen and replied, "I haven't made up my mind yet." It turned out to be the last time I entered a synagogue except as a guest for someone's personal celebration. As unwavering support for the policies of the Israeli government became more and more a "condition" of being Jewish-American, I became increasingly estranged from that community. I saw no more reason to blindly trust the Israeli government than I did to trust the U.S. Government.

On April 28, 1968, the National Mobilization Against the War staged a march in Chicago (and other cities). We gathered in Grant Park and the route would take us through Downtown Chicago and to the Federal Building. There had been several marches before and, while we did not participate in the planning, CADRE members did join the march.

There were many women who were members of the Resistance. Even though they could not go to jail for induction refusal, women were part of the leadership of the organization. The most prominent of these was Joan Baez, whose husband, David Harris, had helped found the organization with friends and colleagues from the Stanford University community. CADRE also had its women members, who ranged from seasoned antiwar veterans to younger girls who were drawn, as we all were, by the heady atmosphere of "sex, drugs and politics" that surrounded our activities. All of us met in the park that Saturday morning to begin what we thought would be another loud but uneventful Peace March in Chicago.

The cops went berserk. Not only did they attack the marchers, they started beating shoppers coming out of Marshall Fields department store on State St. At one point I found myself running down Wabash Avenue, being chased by a cop with his billy club swinging, and protecting one of the younger women who were part of the CADRE contingent. I put myself between her and the cop, who hit me a few times and then ran off after someone else. We went back to my place to recover.

It was clear that the "police riot," as even the Chicago newspapers were forced to call it, was meant to send a message to people around the country that it would be bad for one's health to come to Chicago for the Democratic Party convention in August.. The city was abuzz with debate about police tactics. The leadership of the movement, those who had called the March, decided to stage another march to show that we would not be intimidated by these "Nazi tactics." So, they sat down in the Mayor's office with the police to draw up plans for this new event.

Of course, this next march went off without a hitch. The police showed how civilized they were, the papers stopped discussing "police brutality," and when the actual convention happened the Chicago, police once again became the Chicago police we knew and did not love.

It had been obvious to me that this was the way events would unfold. I could not believe that the organizers would be stupid enough to provide the city and the police with this opportunity for public rehabilitation. I was so disgusted that I joined some friends for a car expedition to California (eight hippies in a Volkswagen bus) that would take me out of town when the next march would take place.

We arrived in Berkeley in the midst of one or another of the ongoing confrontations between the students/young people and the Berkeley police. I went to the Resistance house, where I knew I could find a place to crash, and arranged to meet up with my traveling companions for the return trip to Chicago. Over the next few days, action heated up and a rumor began to circulate that the Resistance house was going to be raided. The problem was that no one there knew where any and all contraband was stashed, and people decided that the best thing to do was simply leave the building for a while. One of the guys came from Southern California, and he decided to go down to LA to escape the heat. I had never been there and decided to join him. I had a friend, David, from my University days who lived in Venice and I figured I could stay with him and his girlfriend, Jennifer.

Jennifer had also been a UofC student. Her older sister, Bernadette, was one of the founders of the Weathermen (or Weather People), one of the most radical of the groups coming out of Students for a Democratic Society. She later married Bill Ayers and came to wider public attention again because of their association with Barack Obama before his election in 2008. David and Jennifer were not "political," but they were sympathetic and welcomed me to their cottage near the beach.

I called Lou from there and he said that he knew a girl from high school who had moved to Southern California and was living near the beach. She lived in Manhattan Beach, several miles south of Venice. I called her and she invited me down. She was a grade school teacher. The school year had just ended and she was ready for some fun. We spent the next several days together. I knew that the people I had come to California with were going to be camping in Big Sur before returning to Chicago, and she suggested that we drive up the Coast and see if we could find them at one of the camp sites in the area. This was not as absurd as it sounds. There were only three or four camp grounds in Big Sur and they would be a pretty conspicuous group—especially as we had tied a cow's skull we found in the Texas desert to the front of the camper. Still, we did not find them and returned to Los Angeles that night. She then decided that it would be a good time to go back to Chicago for a while and see her family and old friends, so we drove back together and arrived at the end of June, 1968.

RED HAIRED ANGEL
(BUSTED FOR REAL)

When I became active in CADRE, I gave up my part in the pot business that had provided me with a stable income. I felt that my participation in the Resistance movement meant that I should not be "dealing drugs," as it would reflect badly on the Movement if I got caught. The result was a slow descent into poverty. I moved out of Lou's and my place and ended up crashing at an apartment rented by a CADRE supporter named Emily. It was near Armitage and Sheffield on the lower rent part of the Near North Side, right where the El trains exited the tunnel from downtown and become elevated again. They roared by every few minutes and the place shook when they passed.

The apartment was located above a Puerto Rican grocery store. When we went up the stairs we would open the door, turn on the lights and then retreat back into the hallway. This allowed the cockroaches to scurry out of sight before we entered. Still, the rent was right (she let me stay for free) and, with the Convention coming soon, I was not interested in wasting time earning money. I was, for all intents and purposes, a "Street Hippie."

Back in 1966, at the end of my senior year at the University of Chicago, a young woman had appeared on the scene.

She was, in my eyes, the quintessential "hippie chick." She had just returned from Europe and North Africa, was slender and beautiful, with eyes that spoke of knowledge far beyond my scope. And she had long red hair that fell to her waist. I was smitten.

I knew, of course, that she was way out of my league. A law school-bound student, even one who smoked pot, was not someone she would be into. Still, I admired her—if not from afar, from far enough away that it felt like a chasm.

She left as mysteriously as she had appeared and I forgot about her. Now, walking down the street in Chicago in July of 1968, I saw her again. She vaguely remembered me and we talked for a while. She asked me if I knew anyone who would have a large quantity of LSD for sale, as she knew someone who wanted to buy in bulk. I did not, but smooth operator that I was, I told her I would keep my eyes open and suggested that she give me her phone number so I could call her if anything came up.

The very next day I ran into some old friends I had not seen in more than a year. They told me that they had a lot of LSD and asked if I "knew anyone who might be interested." This was my chance to replenish my badly depleted resources and gave me a reason to make that call.

We made the deal. Her customer, she said, was connected to the "Chicago mob," who was interested in seeing how to make money from these new drugs. I sat in her apartment on the ground floor and heard his car come down the alley. I knew there was something off about the whole thing, but I didn't care. I was doing this and I would see where it went.

I met "Johnny." He was short, with dark hair and blue eyes, and he wore a fedora. He looked like he could be a gangster. He also looked like he could be a cop trying to look like a gangster. We made the exchange and he gave me his phone number to call if I wanted to move some more product. He went away. I gave her share to my dream girl, and went back to Emily's to crash.

This was all happening in July of 1968. People were starting to drift into town in anticipation of the Democratic Convention happening in August. Everyone knew it would be quite a scene. The City of Chicago announced that it would be enforcing the curfew for Lincoln Park that said no one could be in the park after 11:00pm. I had grown up in Chicago and seen many a sunrise over Lake Michigan from that park—not because I'm an early riser, I just didn't get to sleep last night. This curfew was just something they were making up in order to have a pretext to kick people out of the park and make sure they didn't camp there. There were classes on non-violent tactics given by people who had worked in the Civil Rights Movement. There were people who were mad about the war and people who just wanted to meet other people like them. One afternoon I followed a man with a guitar case into Lincoln Park. I knew he looked familiar, but I couldn't place him. He sat down, took out his guitar and started singing. It was Phil Ochs—the songwriter whose "I Ain't Marchin' Any More" had replaced his "Draft Dodger Rag" as my personal theme song.

On August 20, a week before the DNC began, the Soviet Union invaded Czechoslovakia. There had been a antiwar march planned for that day and it was decided that we should also demonstrate in front of the Soviet Embassy in Chicago, to show that we opposed invasions by any country—not just the United States in Vietnam. Along the way we developed a new tactic. The Chicago Police were notorious for being a nepotism ridden and corrupt institution, filled with cops who knew little or nothing about policing. They were also very out of shape. Our march was accompanied by a large contingent of police, and we decided to begin running in the middle of the march. We would run for a block or two, for no apparent reason, then slow down and let the police catch up. Many of them looked like they might collapse from the effort. Then we would walk for a while and do it again. I don't think anyone dropped dead, but it was a little revenge for the beatings and abuse we had received from the department.

Another afternoon I came back to Emily's. One of the guys from CADRE had brought a bunch of people who had just arrived in town over to the apartment. There, siting on the bed, was Ruth. As soon as I saw her, the red-headed girl was gone from my mind.

Ruth had a Jewish surname, but looked like a WASP princess. Her father was a squat, overweight Jewish doctor and her mom was from an old New England family. She got her mom's looks, but just a little shorter.

We spent the whole convention together. In the park, outside the Hilton Hotel where we organized another bonfire of draft cards burning, driving around Chicago rescuing people—everywhere, it was Ruth and I. She was just 16, but she could run with the best of us. At some point her father showed up. Not to collect her, but to participate in the demonstrations.

The night of August 28, the national guard had established an encampment in the parking area across from the Hilton Hotel, between the outer drive and Michigan Avenue. We had taken some people to a safe place in the city and were returning to the protests outside the Hilton. I found a place to park in an area east of the Guard encampment. We walked peacefully through their area on the way back and rejoined the group in front of the hotel. As we sat down I had this overwhelming feeling that we were all actors in a play, us and the national guardsmen, all playing our part in a life-size surreal drama.

When the convention ended I went back to Westchester County with Ruth and stayed at the family home. It was an old house, just steps from the Hudson River. There were four children in the family and everything was always in chaos. I was a 23 year old, long-haired political radical sleeping with their not-yet 16 year old daughter in her room. Nobody blinked and life went on. We made plans for me to return to Chicago and then come back to New York to be there while Ruth finished her last year of high school. I wasn't going to live with the family, but we would be together in some way.

When I got back to Chicago I needed to raise some cash for the move. I called the number Johnny had given me. It was an answering service and they said he would call back. When he did, I arranged another sale of LSD. It went off without a hitch. I arranged to do it a third and last time. Johnny had asked me if I could get him amphetamines and I had refused, saying "speed kills, man. I wouldn't give speed to anyone. Acid, that's good stuff. Opens your head up." He said he would take the Acid.

I had arranged for a drive-away car to New York. My final sale was set for the morning of that day. It was a Friday, late in September of 1968. I told Johnny to meet me at the back entrance of the building where my parents lived. I was staying at their place until I left the city. From there I would pick up the drive-away and get out of town. He arrived, got out of the car and said "I've got some bad news for you. I'm a DEA agent and you are under arrest."

"Bummer Johnny" was my reply.

At that point two more agents jumped out of the car. They handcuffed me behind my back and threw me into the car. We drove downtown to the Federal Building and went up to their office. They took off the handcuffs and pushed me down in a chair. Johnny said "It will go a lot easier for you if you tell us where you got the stuff. "

"You know I can't do that," I replied.

He went over, picked up the phone and said "We've got a stand up guy here. Come and get him."

At that moment, I understood the meaning of Existentialism—the world view I had read so much about in the work of Jean Paul Sartre and, especially, Albert Camus. People of my generation asked each other "what would you do in this situation or in that one? "Would you have fought in World War II?" "Would you kill in order to protect someone you love?" "Would you rat out a friend to save yourself?" These questions cannot be answered abstractly—they are answered in the moment you exist in that situation. Would I go to Yale or would I not? I had answered that only on the morning of registration. "Would I rat out a friend?" Now I knew the answer to that one. I was happy with my answer—even if I wished it hadn't been asked.

Next they took me to Cook County jail. There is no Federal Lock up in Chicago, but they do have their own section in County, so I was not thrown in with the regular prison population. It was Friday afternoon by now and nothing would happen until Monday morning. I am alone in a cold jail cell in my tee-shirt. As far as I knew, nobody knew I was there. I don't remember if I wasn't offered a phone call or if I declined to use it, but I had not called anyone. I was brought a bologna sandwich on white bread for dinner. That would be every meal between then and when I got out, and I would never eat another one. My life seemed to have gone down the toilet.

Saturday night I was told I had a visitor. It was a lawyer. Some people who knew my parents saw the bust go down (the back entrance to the building is on a small, but busy street). They told my parents. My parents immediately called someone from the Democratic Party who recommended this lawyer. That is who was sitting opposite me when I get into the visitors' room. He told me that sale of LSD is only a misdemeanor, as it has not yet been reclassified as a Class I drug on the Federal Schedule. He said "the max on this is a year, and you should be able to do that standing on your head."

On the way back to my cell, we went by a two-person cell with four black men locked inside. I suggested to the guard that they move one of them in with me to alleviate the overcrowding. He looked at me like I am crazy and told me to "shut up or I'll throw you in with them." I went back to my cell to await the bail hearing on Monday morning. With nothing to read and nothing to do, I passed the time thinking about Ruth and the red-head. I realize that my dream girl had been using me. She must have gotten busted and pointed to me as her "connection" to get a better deal for herself. I also understood why the agent kept trying to get me to sell him speed. A misdemeanor bust would do nothing for his career. Even though I had not thought about my sentence, drug trafficking, in my mind, was associated with a long stretch in prison. The fact that in this case it was a misdemeanor changed everything, and I felt a huge weight taken off my shoulders. I knew that, somehow, everything was going to be all right.

WINTER IS OVER

So it was that I found myself in the Federal Courtroom in Chicago on that cloudy and cold day in early March of 1969.

My lawyer had worked hard during the prior six months to arrange a deal with the prosecution. He pointed out that I was a good Jewish boy and a University of Chicago graduate. The prosecutor replied "Who do you think is selling the drugs in Chicago these days?" Ultimately, they agreed on a year's probation on each count if I plead guilty. I probably could have gotten two of the three charges dropped on the basis of entrapment, since the agent could have arrested me after the first sale and instead tried to get me to sell him a felony drug such as Amphetamines. Still, had I chosen that route, the prosecution would have gone for jail time on the one count and so I went along with my lawyer's recommendation.

The scene in the courtroom was a little bizarre. The judge, who was the only Republican on the Bench in Chicago, pushed the prosecution to go for jail time. He hated these long-hairs who were ruining the country. The prosecutor was put in the awkward position of defending me, and the judge insisted on giving me the maximum he could without sending me to prison: A year on each count, a $1,000 fine on each count, and 5 months in a Federal half-way house. If he couldn't send me to jail, he would do whatever he could to make my life miserable. Later, he himself went to prison when it became public that he was taking bribes from organized crime.

As I stood up to hear my sentence pronounced,, my parents handed me the envelope with my brother's letter. Here, at the low point of my life, perhaps I would be open and receptive to some advice from my stable sibling. They looked expectantly at me as I read the contents. I stood silently for a moment then crumpled it up and threw it away. I shook my head and said "What a bunch of crap." The judge pronounced his sentence and we walked out of the courtroom. I didn't say anything more, but I knew I then I was going to have to change my name. I wasn't an "Edward" and I was never going to be one.

My sentence was set to begin on March 21, 1969—the first day of Spring. About 10 days before that I received a letter from my draft board. It was a notice to report for a new physical exam. This was the first step in the process of going to jail for refusing induction. The date for the new physical was March 21. My parents were *plotzing* (Yiddish for having a conniption). What was I going to do?

I thought about this long and hard. On the one hand, I had pledged to myself that I would go the distance for my opposition to the War and for my personal liberation. On the other hand, I was already in the Federal Prison System. Did I really want to pile one offense on top of the other?

In the end, I decided on a compromise. I went into a phone booth and called my draft board. I explained my predicament to the little old lady who answered the phone. I said that I could not be in two places at once, even for the

Federal Government, and I had decided that the Bureau of Prisons had a stronger claim on my body than the draft board. She asked me to send them a letter explaining the situation but I refused, saying that it was hard enough for me to make this phone call, and it was up to them to do what they decided to do. A few weeks later another envelope came from the draft board. In it was a new draft card with a 4F classification. The government had decided that they did not want me under any circumstances. My parents wondered what I would do. In the end, I threw the card into a drawer and, a few days later, reported to the Halfway House located in the Downtown Chicago YMCA. My Redheaded Angel had saved me from three years in a Federal prison.

I was in the halfway house for two days. At that point I was called into the Director's office. He verified that I came from Chicago and asked if I had a place to live here. I replied that I could always stay at my parents' house. He said that they needed my room for someone coming out of prison who needed to ease his way into the community, and told me that as long as I called in every day and came in three times a week to sign the book, they did not want to see me again. I agreed to these terms and left the Y.

That summer, Ruth came out from New York to live with me in Chicago. We found a little place on the near North Side, not far from where we had met. I was driving my father's Stella D'oro cookie truck without a license and living with an underage girl while under the supervision of the Federal Bureau of Prisons. Still, I called every day and showed up three times a week at the office. Late one night in the middle of that summer, my parents called me in a panic. The halfway house had called, saying that I had not reported by phone that day and demanding to speak with me. I immediately called them back. I told them that I had called at lunch time, and that the director of the program himself had answered the phone. Clearly, he had answered from his office and neglected to go out to where the book was kept and mark in that I had called, They had me hold on while they woke him to verify this and then apologized and let me go back to sleep. This was as close as I came to getting caught in violation of the terms of my sentence.

On August 20 my five months were up. I went to visit my probation officer in the Federal Building. He was an old Leftist who had found a place for himself in the Federal Bureaucracy and loved us young radicals. I told him I wanted to get out of Chicago and asked him for permission to travel for a couple of months to decide where I wanted to settle to do the rest of my probation. He agreed, as long as I called him every couple of weeks to check in.

Ruth had graduated from High School that June and was set to start college at a small New England Liberal Arts School. I began by going out to visit her (by now it was mid-September). We spent an idyllic week at a cabin owned by a faculty member. During that time I met some people who had a commune in the woods nearby, and I told them I would come back and move in at the end of my trip. Ruth and I went back to Westchester to visit with her folks. We also went down to Columbia University. My old friend Doug had moved back to New York and was tending bar near the school. I introduced him to Ruth and he asked me if I was planning to adopt her. By then, his charisma had worn off for me and I said goodbye. A few years later I heard that he had fallen off a roof while high on heroin. I was pretty sure he had jumped.

I also spent a night with Judy, who had moved to New York for Graduate School. That night we recapitulated our entire relationship, from early passion to bitter recrimination. I was so happy to return to Ruth and continue building my new life. A few days later her siblings drove me to the New York State Through-way to begin my trip to and across Canada and down to Southern California, where I could again stay with my friends in Venice.

My first stop was in Toronto, a hot bed of radical politics and counter-cultural action. I crashed with some people who lived in the Towers. From there I got a ride all the way to Suie St, Marie, Ontario, the gateway to Lake Superior. I arrived in Suie St Marie after dark and was let off at a gas station just west of the city, It was also a stop for the Greyhound Bus, and I figured I could take a bus through the night to get closer to Regina, where I planned to spend a week with my friend Kevin, who had worked with me in CADRE and had returned to Canada (he had dual citizenship) rather than be drafted.

Sault Ste. Marie is a place of very changeable and extreme weather. This particular night in October was cold as could be, or even colder. They told me that the Greyhound would be at this stop in a couple of hours. In the meantime, the station closed and I huddled near the building, hoping not to freeze before the bus came. When the time was right, I moved to the highway and waited under the lights. The bus sped by me, never even slowing down. At this point I remembered there was a small motel back down the road. I put my backpack on and struggled to get to the building. I rang the bell for a long time before someone came to the desk. He looked at me standing outside the door and finally buzzed me into the lobby. "I need a room for the night," I said to him. He looked at me for a minute and replied "We don't have rooms for people like you." I wanted to point out to him that this was what the innkeeper had told Joseph, but instead I very calmly pulled out my wallet and said "Look I have cash money for the room, and if you don't rent to me, I will probably die of exposure on your doorstep." He rented me the room and even threw in an alarm clock so I could get up at dawn and continue my hitchhike west. Saved by Canadian civility.

Morning broke clear and somewhat warmer. I got back on the highway and stuck my thumb out. The first car that came along stopped for me. It was a doctor in a Cadillac. He was driving all the way around Lake Superior and was happy to have the company and the chance to meet a real live hippie. We had a great time and saw some of the most beautiful scenery I had ever experienced. Huge trees and crystal lakes, a great lunch and wonderful conversation. I have probably hitchhiked 20,000 miles in my life and this was the best ride of all time.

I spent a week with Kevin and continued my westward trek. I soon found myself in the middle of Alberta, standing along a desolate Highway 1 and trying to keep out of the way of the tumbleweeds that rolled down the road. I also tried to keep out of the way of the pick-up trucks with the gun racks that answered my outstretched thumb by running me off the side of the highway. Alberta, I discovered, was the Texas of Canada—cattle, oil and hatred of hippies. Also endless prairies. I finally got a ride that took me all the way to Banff, gateway to the Canadian Rockies.

I had been left off in the middle of the night and thrown my sleeping bag on the side of the road. When

I awoke in the morning it was in the midst of tall trees and towering mountains, a place of incredible beauty. Again, the hitchhiking Gods had taken good care of me.

The rest of the trip was uneventful. I hitched to Vancouver, BC and then down into Washington State. There I was told that hitchhiking on the highway was illegal, and that the State Police enforced this rigorously. I took the only bus of the entire journey, from Seattle to Portland, OR. I continued hitchhiking down Hwy 5 through California and into Los Angeles. My last ride was with a guy going from Sacramento to LA in an old pick-up. We had to cross over from the 5 to the 101 as his truck could not make it up the Grapevine into LA County. Indeed, it hardly made it up the Camarillo Grade into the San Fernando Valley. We had to stop twice on the way up so that the truck wouldn't overheat.

During the ride he told me he was going to be working at a restaurant in West Hollywood, and when I told him that I had experience as a cook he assured me that I would also be able to find work there.

I arrived in Venice just after New Years of 1970. I went to the Beach and lay on the warm sands. I realized that there was no way I was going back to New England to live in a commune in the woods. Ruth could come and spend the Summer in California, but for me, Winter was over.

PART III

CALIFORNIA

WELCOME TO LOS ANGELES, CITY OF TOMORROW

People come to California to reinvent themselves, or to allow their real selves to emerge. This was even more the case in 1970, when it was virtually impossible, for instance, to be gay in small town America. Or to not be someone's son or daughter, with the expectation that this would define one's life. Almost everyone was from somewhere else—and if they were not, it was likely that their parents or grandparents were. In Southern California, many of these people had come to be in the movies. Most, of course, had failed to achieve this goal. Still, they brought their good looks with them, and passed this on to their children. The result was that I saw more beautiful women every day than I had seen in my whole life in Chicago.

For me, it was not so much a question of "re-inventing" myself, but of figuring out who I was and who I was going to be. I was no longer a super-smart, upwardly mobile Jewish lawyer-to-be. I couldn't be a full time political radical organizer while on probation, and I was not even sure that was what I wanted to do. I did know that I didn't want to be "Eddie" anymore, but aside from that there was nothing leading me in one direction or another.

First, however, I needed to get settled. I needed work to support myself and also as a condition of probation. And I needed a place to live.

Today, Venice Beach is the second most visited tourist destination in Southern California—beaten only by Disneyland. Back then, it was a sleepy little beach town. Home to old Jewish people, the last of the Beats and a bunch of young hippies. There were Black people who lived there and Latinos too. It was affordable housing near the water. The beach itself was the "poor people's beach," since it was easily accessible from the Eastern part of LA via the Venice Blvd. Bus, which traveled all the way from East LA with its last stop just a few blocks from the sand. The canals had turned to marshes and there were no movie stars or million dollar homes in the neighborhood. There were a lot of little bungalows, and I found mine on Palms Blvd. near Oakwood Ave., less than a mile from the water.

I had been to California three times before. The first time was with a couple of guys I knew from the University of Chicago. Steve D. was a student a year or so behind me. He came from a wealthy family and when his father died he decided to invest some of his inheritance in California pot and bring it back to Chicago to sell. Rick, on the other hand, was a Creole who hung around the University, playing pool and hanging out with the students. During this summer of 1966, we decided to go along with Steve for the ride and visit the West Coast. Steve got a car and we set out for San Francisco to score.

This was a year before the "Summer of Love." Height-Asbury was emerging, but it was pretty gritty and had something of an East Village feel to it. Steve quickly got burnt in his deal and disappeared—leaving Rick and I stranded in Northern California without enough money to even get a bus home. It was a long way to hitch-hike and the prospects were not that great for a white and black guy traveling together. Rick had never hitched, and not surprisingly, was not keen to try. We had enough to buy bus tickets to Reno, where we thought we would try to parlay our remaining cash at the tables to get us home. Within an hour of arriving we were broke, down to our last dollar. I had a gas credit card from my father. We used it to get a cheap motel room and a candy bar. We called our friend Doug (collect) in Chicago and he agreed to wire us $100. It was not enough to get us home, but we thought we would go back to the tables and try again.

This time the travel Gods were with us. We both started winning at Blackjack. We switched to Craps and won there as well. We even came close to winning the pick 8 Jackpot at Keno, scoring 6 of the first 10 numbers, but petering out in the second half and settling for a small return. By lunchtime we had enough to pay for train tickets to Chicago, with money left over to pay Doug back and have some to live on for a while. We left the tables, had something to eat and went to a local pool hall to wait for train time. We even beat some of the locals at 9-ball. It was the best day of gambling in my life. When it was over, I hardly ever gambled again—at least for money.

The second trip to California was in December, 1967. It was after the Pentagon Demonstration and before I began working with CADRE. I had money from our pot-selling business and friends who had already moved West. I flew out to San Francisco and spent New Years East at the Fillmore, listening to some of the legendary San Francisco rockers of that era—although which ones, I don't remember. I know it wasn't Janis, but who it was has disappeared into the mists of memory. At any rate, I returned to a sub-zero Chicago on New Years Day of 1968. I had left my keys at home and when I got to the door there was a note from Lou saying he would be back soon. I waited in a freezing doorway down the street. It was a few hours before his return. During that time I also remembered another freezing day a few years before. I had my father's car on the South Side, and needed to get it back to him in the morning. When I came out to the car the door locks had frozen. There was a guy driving around with battery cables selling jump starts to stranded motorists. I was finally able to get some boiling water to defrost the locks, managed to get the car out of the ice-encrusted parking spot and drive back to my parents' apartment on the North Side. That memory, and the stark contrast between my current condition in the doorway way and the weather in San Francisco the day before convinced me that California was the place for me.

The last time I went was in late May of 1968. This was the trip I described earlier, when I had ended up in LA after fleeing Berkeley and the Resistance house. Now I was returning to the Southland to do my probation on the Beach.

After a day or so of acclimation, I rode a motorbike lent by a friend of a friend up to the Cafe Figaro, located on the Western edge of Melrose Ave., near Robertson Blvd. Cafe Figaro was a transplanted institution from Greenwich Village in Manhattan. The owner wanted to move to LA, and he brought the Cafe with him. I spoke with the manager and told him about my experience managing a coffee house in Hyde Park, near the University of Chicago. He said they did not have an opening, but he would call me when and if he did. A few minutes after I got back to Venice, the phone rang. It was the manager calling to ask if I could start work that night. I got back on the bike and returned to West Hollywood. The Cafe Figaro was a sprawling spot. It was open from about 11:00 a.m. to 1:00 a.m. Everyone who worked there (with the exception of the night manager, a one-armed artist who became a friend) was an aspiring actor. All the waitresses were beautiful, the waiters handsome, and even the cooks were in the biz. On the night shift cooking with me were Chuck and Hans. Chuck was a 6-foot-7 African American who mostly played "heavies" when he got roles. Hans was a diminutive blond German who looked like a Nazi. They did not get along. I was the long-haired hippie who stood between them at the stoves and ovens.

The house specialty drink was Sangria punch, which was made in bulk and kept in a large trash can in the kitchen. The wait staff just dipped their pitchers in and served it to the customers. Everyone on staff was allowed to drink it as well. We also passed joints around during the long hours of food prep. By the end of the night, it was a miracle that anyone got their orders done right.

Tom Ziegler, the owner, was a drunk—and an offensive one at that. After hours he would often chase the waitresses around the restaurant, trying to cop a feel. He bought a boat and would invite the employees on board once or twice a year to listen to his stories and drink. This made it an asset of the business and tax-deductible. I went once—I sat at the bow, looked at the ocean and ignored the scene behind me.

In March a contingent from Max's Kansas City in New York came to play softball with us. It was something the restaurants had done before Cafe Figaro moved, and we were told they wanted to revive the tradition. The owners wanted to hang out and escape the New York winter, and this was a way to make it a business expense.

On the day before the game we gathered for practice. We were joined by one non-employee who was a partner in the business and a friend of Tom's. It was Bill Cosby. It was before The Cosby Show and the Jello commercials, when he was just a pretty successful stand-up comedian. He played shortstop and joined Tom in his pursuit of the waitresses, one of whom ultimately joined the parade of lawsuits around Cosby's predatory sexual activities.

By this time I was tired of working at the restaurant. I knew I should be driving a Taxi, and it was only inertia and the beautiful waitresses that were keeping me at Figaro's. Fortunately, the decision was made for me.

One evening, the manager called the night shift cooks together. He told us that Tom wanted to "experiment" with keeping the restaurant open until 3:00 a.m., 2 hours later than its current closing time. However, because it was an experiment, we would not be paid for the two extra hours "yet." I instantly replied "yes, but aren't we working now?." When I got home, I got a call telling me I was fired.

CALL ME A CAB

When people think of Los Angeles, they picture this huge city, spreading out in all directions over Southern California. This is true, but incomplete. The city of Los Angeles contains, within its boundaries, several independent municipalities. Beverly Hills and Santa Monica are only two of these. There are also unincorporated areas that are included in the county of Los Angeles, but not in the city. The independent cities have their own government, and license their own taxi companies. After checking out the choices, I decided to join Yellow Cab of Culver City.

Culver City is located between Venice and Mar Vista (which are part of the City of LA) to the West and the rest of the city to the East. It is between Beverly Hills to the North and Los Angeles International Airport to the south. It is sort of nowhere, but close to everything.

The cab company was located on Robertson Blvd., about ¾ of a mile North of Venice Blvd. I decided to work days, since I did not know the area as well as I had in Chicago, and it would be easier to navigate during daylight. I could catch the bus up Venice Blvd and transfer to the bus going North on Robertson for an easy early morning commute, since my borrowed motor bike had to be returned to its owner.

The story of how Los Angeles lost its public transportation system to a consortium of automobile, tire and oil companies is an oft-told one. I lived out this story on a daily basis. I would go east on the 6:15 a.m. bus. As we would approach Robertson Blvd., the Northbound Bus would usually pull away just before we arrived. Since transfers were not free, I never knew whether to buy one or not. I would wait until we were very close to Robertson to make my decision. If I missed the Northbound bus, I had to walk the three-quarters of a mile to the garage, as the next bus did not come soon enough to avoid being late to work. I called the bus company several times to ask why they did not hold the bus for the extra 30 seconds or a minute that would allow for transfers. They gave me a different reason every time I called, but ultimately I had to give up and buy a motorcycle. I never used public transportation again.

The taxi business in Los Angeles was and is very different than in Chicago or other large cities. Almost all of it is via radio calls, except for cab stands at hotels and the airport. Few residents use taxis on a regular basis. The poor struggle with the inadequate public transit system and everyone else (including many of the poor), has a car. If someone is hailing a cab, they are generally an out-of-towner who does not know better. It took me a little while to figure out how to make a living driving here, but it was high stress work, and even though I was doing all right, I wanted to find something else. I was in California now, and I felt like driving for a living was too much like Chicago. At the same time, I did not want a career and would never work for a corporation. If I was going to work within the existing system using my brain, I should have gone to Yale and become rich doing it. I had to find another path.

When I first arrived in Los Angeles I went to the Federal building downtown to report to the probation department and meet my new supervisor. He was a hard-ass, unlike my old Lefty officer in Chicago, and he could not believe that I had been allowed to leave the country and travel around for three months without supervision.

He reminded me that I had to find a job and make payments on my fine and made it plain that he was not going to be easy to get along with. I did not want to pay this fine. I did not want any of my money going to the Federal Government to help them fight their illegal and immoral war. I realized that I was going to have to have a good reason not to be working and paying off this $3,000. After thinking about the problem I came to the conclusion that going back to school was the only way out. I resisted this thought for a while. I had hated school and couldn't believe I was contemplating returning. The more I thought about it, the more I could see how different it could be. To begin with, I had a real, concrete reason to be in school, which was quite different from the aimless way it had been before. Second, instead of being at the University of Chicago, which was in Chicago, I would be on a beautiful campus, near the ocean, in Southern California. Third, while UCLA was a fine school, it was not the intellectually pretentious and competitive atmosphere of the proto-Ivy League UofC. UCLA had the best basketball team in the country (I had always loved basketball), lots of music and other free or cheap activities. And, finally, even though I would have to keep driving a cab to pay my rent and expenses, as a graduate student I would be eligible for assistantships or other jobs through the university that could get me out of the cab at some point. I convinced myself—I would become a student again.

I didn't want to continue in Sociology. I hated the field. Everyone spoke in jargon and created huge studies to prove things that were either obvious or not useful to know. I realized that American History was not only the most interesting, but also the easiest subject for my reentry into academic life. I called UCLA, but they said that the deadline for entering in the Fall had just closed and I would have to wait a year to apply.

Another thing I had done when I arrived in Los Angeles was to make contact with Irv White, my old boss at Creative Research Associates in Chicago. He had moved to LA to open a branch there. He actually wanted to start writing screenplays and working in film. Also, he and his partner had stopped getting along, and it was not long before they split the company. Irv was trying to downsize the business in order to find time to do his creative work, and I began a long-term relationship where he could call on me when he needed help, at much less cost than having a full-time employee. For my part I could earn far more working for him than any other part-time job I would be able to find. This relationship went on for many years and played a crucial part in my future. In the meantime, I made a nice connection to his secretary, with whom I also had a relationship for several years. Debbie was divorced and had a young daughter—she was the first woman I had ever dated who had a child. I felt quite grown up. For the first time I thought about having children in the future.

When I told Irv about my plan to go back to school and having to wait a year to apply, he told me that his neighbor was the head of the History department and he would speak to him on my behalf. I got my interview. The professor who interviewed me specialized in Labor History. I was the first person he had ever interviewed who had actually been a union member. I told him the story of the Teamsters, the Longshoremen and the taxi drivers. He was fascinated by my knowledge of the situation.

I was also a member of the Wobblies (Industrial Workers of the World), whose national headquarters were a few blocks from my apartment in Chicago. The Wobblies were a legendary union of the early 20th century, whose organizers included Joe Hill. Joe was framed for murder while organizing miners in Utah. His famous last words, uttered before the firing squad, were "don't mourn—organize." He was the subject of many songs and stories, including "I dreamed I saw Joe Hill last night," which Joan Baez had sung. The Wobblies were not active anymore as a union. I had joined out of respect and nostalgia. This sealed the deal for me with the professor. I was a student again.

RUN FOR YOUR LIFE

After my acceptance I checked out the campus. It was huge and beautiful. It had a botanical and a sculpture garden, a huge student activities center, movie theater and athletic facilities. It also had the newly constructed Sunset recreation center featuring two pools, beach volleyball courts and a mind-numbing number of gorgeous young women wearing almost no clothing at all. On the one hand I felt like I had died and gone to heaven, and on the other I was totally intimidated. I had no (or perhaps very few) illusions about my looks. I was a long-haired, bearded hippie. Some women would like that, some wouldn't. The problem was my body. I was in the shape you would expect from someone who had smoked cigarettes since the age of eleven and hadn't played sports since high school pick-up games. I had played around with weights off and on and dieted several times, but the results were what you would expect. Not pretty. I realized that I would have to get serious if I intended to play in the league I wanted to play in. It was true that I had a girlfriend "back east," but Ruth and I understood that abstinence was a crime against both of our natures, and any attempt or expectation in that regard would only break us up as a couple. I also understood that Ruth and I had a soul connection transcending her being so much better looking than me. Potential sexual partners would be a different story. I immediately started watching my food intake and working out at the men's gym. I was making progress, but it wasn't fast enough. I had to bite the bullet—quit smoking and start running. I devised a unorthodox method of leaving tobacco behind. Every time I just had to have a cigarette, I would smoke a joint instead. I was higher more often, but it helped me get through the worst of the nicotine withdrawals. When I had started smoking weed, I understood that if I gave into the munchies, I would ultimately weigh 300 pounds, so I had never made eating a part of the smoking experience. Often, I would feel more body awareness when I was high, which was a good incentive to not eat.

As soon as I quit, I went out to the running track across from the men's gym. I had never been on a track before. Like all tracks, it was a quarter-mile oval. The first day, I got half way around and collapsed in a heap. I went back every day. Within a few months I could run a mile, and then two and three. I began doing wind sprints followed by walking and then more sprints. Within a year I was running around the campus on a cross country trail that began with a steep climb up from Westwood Ave. along Sunset Boulevard, breathing the exhaust from the cars as you climbed. My run was about five miles in length, ending with a lap at top speed around the track where I had begun my running career.

Some days I ran along the beach. There was a measured mile, with quarter miles marked on the lifeguard towers, between Pico Boulevard and the Santa Monica Pier. I ran barefoot on the hard sand. When I got a dog, she ran with me. I would start off slowly, cruise at good speed for miles three and four, and try to sprint as much of the last mile as possible, ending at maximum speed and then walking for another half mile to cool down. On my best early morning run, someone asked me if I was training for the Olympics.

Lifting weights outdoors in Venice was a lot of fun. Today, Muscle Beach is an important part of the Venice scene. It features modern equipment and a large bleacher where people can watch the bodybuilders show off—either in competitions or just working out. In the early '70s, it was known as "The Pit"—a small enclosure with a low fence, a few pieces of equipment and assorted free weights. It was operated as a club by the parks department, with dues set at $12 per year. This was done to keep the inebriated and casually high people from coming in to fool around with the weights and hurt themselves. Arnold Schwarzenegger and a few other big names would come over from Gold's gym to lift on the beach from time to time, but otherwise it was a very quiet but beautiful place to work out. Sometimes a woman would come to watch and, perhaps, invite one of us home. There was one serious and seriously beautiful woman who worked out with us, but otherwise it was a male preserve.

The pinnacle of my physical fitness came when I could play basketball with the football players, who came into Pauly Pavilion to play half-court during the off-season. These were seriously big guys, eight or nine years younger than me, and most of them taller. Plus, they were real athletes—college football players. I loved sports, especially basketball, but I was never any good. I just liked the game. Now I was fighting for rebounds with the football players. It was a real kick.

I also met a real-life surfer dude. He took me out to Malibu to experience the sport with him. I spent about 4 hours lying on a board waiting for a wave that never came, and left with nipples that were sore for weeks. I never returned for a second lesson, but I did become an avid and adventurous body surfer. I loved being in the ocean, especially when the waves were running. The feeling of being caught up in a cresting wave and knowing that you have no choice but to ride it was one of the most exhilarating physical activities I have ever enjoyed. When my first daughter was born I took her into the ocean with me at a young age. She was absolutely fearless and loved diving under the waves. She dreamed that she was a mermaid, and swam with her mermaid friend Crystal during the night. All of her kindergarten friends believed her, and when a new child came into the class and doubted the story, the other children would assure them that it was true. She later learned to scuba dive and is a passionate advocate for water protection, with a Masters in Environmental Studies.

Meanwhile, back in the classroom, my academic career was going well. Almost all of the graduate students in my department had come directly from college. I, on the other hand, had five years of life experience between college graduation and coming back to school. In many ways I was closer in age and outlook with the younger professors in the department. Also, all the other graduate students were looking for careers in academia and obsessed over the work. I was more laid back, knowing that I was "serving my time" here instead of in a prison. In the middle of my first year I applied for a teaching assistantship for the Fall semester. I was accepted. This meant that, for my second and third year, I would be paid to be in school. And, to make it even sweeter, Ronald Reagan would be signing my paycheck. If he only knew…

During that first year I still had to earn some money. My rent was $100 per month and I had a series of roommates to share the costs. Gas was around $0.35 to $0.40 per gallon. I got a used Yamasaki 250 motorcycle for the commute to UCLA. It was the smallest freeway-legal motorcycle. The first time I rode it on the freeway I held the bar in a death grip and my heart was pounding the whole ride. Within a few weeks I was using one hand and checking out the cars and people as I lane-split. I recall one Fall day, riding Eastward on the Santa Monica Freeway. I saw these incredible snow-capped mountains in the distance. It was the first time the Santa Ana winds had pushed the smog out to sea, and the mountains around Los Angeles became visible.

My expenses were very low. I played on the beach or at UCLA, cooked for myself or ate cheap at school, and spent about a dollar a week on gas and oil for the bike. I worked for Culver City Yellow on Friday and Sunday late afternoons into the early morning hours. By this time I was renting the cab from the owner and earned whatever I took in off the meter plus tips. It was certainly enough to live on.

During the summer after my first year I was returning to Chicago to drive my father's truck for him so that my parents could take an extended vacation. It was a good deal for all of us. My parents paid me enough so that I would not have to work too much when I returned home, and they were able to go away knowing that the route would be well taken care of and they would still be earning something while they were gone.

When I drove the cab two days a week, I always deposited my lease fee in a envelope that I put in a slot in the company safe. The last time I drove before going to Chicago, the owner's son was in the office when I returned the cab. He told me I should give him the envelope as he was taking the deposit to the bank in the morning. When I returned to LA, I came in and got my cab. When I brought it back the owner was waiting for me. He said that I had forgotten to drop off the lease payment for the last drive. I told him what had happened, but he said his son did not get my envelope. I understood that he had to believe his son over me, but I just gave him the fee for the current drive and said goodbye. A few years later the company went out of business.

THE NEW ME

Ever since I came to California, I had been thinking, and talking, about changing my name. The process that had begun in the courtroom, when my parents had given me the letter from my brother about my names, was coming to fruition. One of my friends reminded me that in the Fall I would be in front of students who did not know me, and who would address me as I told them to. It would be a "now or never" moment for name changing. So, in the spring of 1972 I went down to the DMV and signed a form that stated I was changing my first name and had no intention of using this for fraudulent purposes. I walked out with a new driver's license with the name Abraham Entin on it. It was as simple as that.

Why Abraham?

When Jewish children are born, they are given an English name and a Hebrew name. Usually, there is a direct connection between the two—the English name being a version of the Hebrew one. My father was named Jacob, which is the English version of Yaacov. Smuel became Samuel, and so on. They are also often named after a deceased relative. There are two versions of why the relative should be deceased. The first is that if the child turns out bad, it will not reflect upon a living person. The second is that, when the Angel of Death comes, he shouldn't take the wrong person.

In my case I was named after my father's father, Abraham, who had died when the depression destroyed his business. In 1945, Jewish parents hesitated to give their child an obviously Jewish name, as anti-Semitism was still very much a reality to them. So, instead of naming me "Abraham," they gave me the name of a recently deceased British monarch. It is not surprising that I never felt comfortable as "Edward," and even "Eddie" just never felt right. So, even though I had stopped believing in Judaism as a religion, I felt very strongly that "Abraham" was my name, and I was going to take it back for myself.

A few weeks after completing the name change, I left for Chicago to work my father's cookie route for him. This was my first return to Chicago since changing my name and my body. I was very curious and a little nervous about how things would go in the old home town. I would be there for 3 weeks. I could run my father's route in three days, when it would take him a week. Aside from being younger and faster, I did not have to socialize with the customers as he enjoyed doing. Go in, take inventory. Go out, make up order. Come in and stock the shelves and move on to the next store. Plus driving to Cicero once a week to stock the truck. I had been doing it for a long time and had it down pat. This would leave me four days a week to play.

I also saw my old friend and partner Lou. He was living with a new woman and working, so we couldn't hang out too much, but he told me his older brother had gotten a pilot's license and would be happy to take me up for a ride. I called him and arranged to meet at Meig's Field, where the private planes were hangared. Barry was notorious for his drinking and drug consumption, but I was pretty sure he was sober for the flight. He had become a math teacher in order to avoid Vietnam, but it turned out he liked it and had settled into a career. We were joined by a female colleague of his, Barbara, who also wanted to experience flying.

We flew south out of Chicago. It was beautiful. On the way back, Barry told me to take over the controls. He pointed out the window to the river below. "Just follow that—it will take you right into Downtown." I piloted the plane for a while and offered the controls to Barry's friend. She declined and I piloted until we we entered Chicago airspace, when Barry wisely took over the controls and landed us safely. We were all very excited. Barry went home to his wife, and Barbara invited me over to her apartment. We transferred our excitement to other activities and I moved into her lovely apartment in the Lincoln Park area. She came from a wealthy family in Highland Park (one of the most expensive of the Chicago suburbs) and one day we went up and hung out at the country club. I was the only long-haired hippie type near the pool, but if she didn't care, neither did I.

I had stayed in touch over the years with my high school girlfriend, Shirley, who also lived in Lincoln Park. We had continued the pattern of our old relationship, with her clearly in control and me left hanging every time. We met for lunch and she made it clear that if I came over that night we would go "all the way."

I went back to Barbara's and explained my predicament to her. I told her I was convinced that the encounter would be disappointing, but after 10 years of dancing around, there was no way I could turn down this opportunity. She told me that if I left that evening, I should not come back.

I left, and it was indeed disappointing. Shirley had gone from being an edgy teenager to a very straight 26 year old. All of the social changes of the past 10 years seemed to have passed her by. She didn't even smoke pot and had never tried it! Still, I was glad to have that fixation and frustration gone, even if it meant returning to my parent's place alone.

Before I had left for Chicago, Debbie, Irv's secretary, had told me she was going to the East Coast around the same time and might be able to stop in Chicago for a couple of days. I gave her the number at my parent's place (long before the days of cell phones), not really expecting her call. She did. She could stop in Chicago for the last three days before my parents returned. I said sure and picked her up at O'Hare a few days later. I took her back to the airport after the three days, hung around for an hour and met my parents' plane. My mother asked me if I had shown my friend all around Chicago during her stay (my mother had become very enthusiastic about her adopted home town). I told her we had not left the bedroom. It was the first time I had ever seen my mother blush, and it ended the conversation. The next day I went home to California, feeling confident in my emerging new self.

In the Fall, when school came back into session, I introduced myself as Abraham. I was very adamant that I was "Abraham." I quickly corrected anyone who called me Abe. I also became very aware of other people and their names, and began to make sure to address people as they introduced themselves, never shortening or calling a Robert "Bob" without them inviting me to do so. It wasn't until years later, when an important customer called me "Abe," that I modified my policy about correcting people.

LOOKING FOR A SIGN

The fact that I had escaped going go jail for my political convictions did not mean I had abandoned them. The events after my arrest had forced me to concentrate on my personal situation, but the war was never far from my mind. When I came to California, I had to figure out how to re-engage in social and political activism in a way that would not violate my probation and get me sent to jail.

The months before the Democratic Convention had left me at odds with many of my fellow protesters. This had begun when CADRE was forced to move out of our donated office space. Where would we go? We had talked a lot about "engaging the community" with our group and movement. A storefront in a nearby, ethnically diverse neighborhood would make us much more visible to many more and differ-ent people. In the end, the group decided on a cheaper space that was upstairs in a small office building, where no one who did not know us would find us there.

Then, of course, there was the stupidity of the "second peace march" that let the cops off the hook for their behavior during the police riot. The fratricidal tendencies of the Left were also blooming at the time. The fracturing of Students for a Democratic Society (SDS), the feuds between Mao-ists, Revolutionary Socialists and the maze of other groups convinced that theirs was the only way forward reminded me of George Orwell's description of the infighting among the International Brigades during the Spanish Civil War, which he described in *Homage to Catalonia*, the account of his personal experiences during that struggle. Now, in my new life, I had to find a way to participate in "revolutionary" work that would be effective, but that would not lead me into prison.

Soon after I arrived in LA, a major demonstration against the war took place in front of the Federal Building in Westwood, not far from UCLA. It was also close to the Veteran's Cemetery. After the formal demonstration was over, a large contingent decided to go to the cemetery and continue the protest against the senseless killing and dying that was filling up graves in Vietnam and the United States. I joined the march to the site, but when the call went out to go inside and risk arrest, I had to disengage. It was the first time I had walked away from political confrontation and it felt very strange.

All of this came to a head for me at the time of the so-called "Christmas bombings." On December 18, 1972, President Nixon, having been reelected in a landslide, ordered a significant increase in the bombing of North Vietnam over the next several weeks. He had no doubt scheduled this at least in part because school would be out and students, the most vocal opponents of the war, would be dispersed around the country, unable to organize mass protests.

The Antiwar groups in Los Angeles called a meeting to discuss strategies on how to maximize our visibility and demonstrate opposition to the escalation of hostilities. I went. I did not know anyone, but "everyone" had been invited to attend. I listened as one group after another made suggestions on where, when and how a protest should be organized. Finally, I raised my hand. I reminded the group that the Super Bowl would take place at the Los Angeles Coliseum on January 14th. The eyes of all America would be there. President Nixon was a big fan and football--war analogies were a favorite of his. If we could mount some kind of action there, perhaps even interfering with this most symbolic American institution, we would be sure to garner a huge amount of publicity for the Movement. For me, it was the University of Chicago Great Football Protest all grown up.

I was met with total silence. No one knew me, and I was not a representative of one group or another. The idea seemed to be so far out of the usual ways of protesting that no one knew how to respond. In the end, no unified plan was adopted and the meeting disintegrated.

I really believed in my idea and I resolved to carry it out—even if I had to act alone. I went to see my friend Monty—the one-armed artist who had been a manager at Figaro's and lived close by me in Venice. I asked him to make me a sign. A very ugly sign—as ugly as he could. I asked him to write "In Vietnam, it is Raining Bombs on People," with red streaks of blood coming down from the letters. He did a great job. Early in the morning of Super Bowl Sunday I drove down to the neighborhood around the Coliseum, parked my old car, walked the several blocks to the remake of the Roman building where Christians had been thrown to the Lions (who were not playing that day) and found a spot to stand with my sign. I had no idea how people would react, but I was bound and determined to stand my ground.

Most people, of course, simply ignored me. Those who did not, however, were intrigued by the fact that I was doing this alone, without a bunch of other people, and that I was not telling them what to do (end the war, etc) but simply reminding them of what else was happening that day. A couple of people who had extra tickets they were planning on scalping even offered to give one to me. I declined, knowing I would have to abandon my sign to get inside. I felt very good about what I had done. When the game began I returned to the car and drove back to Venice.

When school reopened the next week, I decided to continue using my sign. I was already a Teaching Assistant with an office in Bunch Hall—the "Waffle Building" on North Campus. Twice a week I would stand in front of the elevators for a half hour during lunch time, holding my sign. I didn't speak to anyone unless they spoke to me first. Finally, an Asian student came up to me. I wondered what he would ask or say. "Did you know that 'Vietnam' is misspelled on your sign?" I turned it around. Sure enough, the "I" and the "E" had been transposed, but neither I nor anyone else had noticed this before. We had been in the country for almost 10 years, and none of us even knew how to spell its name.

My other political activity, which I had begun soon after arriving in Los Angeles, was supporting the United Farm Workers, led by Caesar Chavez, in their campaign to gain fair wages, working conditions and dignity for the people who planted and picked our crops. This campaign revolved around gaining union representation and a contract from table grape growers in California. This was a high profile campaign, with Robert Kennedy even feeding bread to Caesar Chavez as he ended his 25 day fast on March 10th of 1968—shortly before Kennedy's assassination in June of that year. By this time I understood why "bananas taste like blood" and the human cost of American agricultural practices. I had heard Woody Guthrie's great songs "Deportees" and "Pastures of Plenty," both of which resonated through the lives of Chicanos toiling in the Central Valley of California.

Most of the T.A.'s in the history department were apolitical. Indeed, so were most of the teachers. One of the younger professors, with whom I became somewhat friendly, described it this way to me one afternoon as we smoked a joint together. He had become an academic, he explained, because he "wanted to live in the interstices of life." " Interstice" is defined as "a small space between things," and I have never forgotten this characterization of the academic approach to life. He did not want to engage, but to observe (and comment upon) events in the real world from this "small space between things." I understood, and I was reinforced in my attitude that I was in school to fulfill my probation, and for no other reason.

Two of the more political people in the American History Department were both named "Al." Professor Alexander Saxton was a Harvard student who had come west to California riding in boxcars during the Great Depression. He had authored a series of novels on the lives of working people during that period and ended up becoming a full professor at UCLA. Funny, warm and engaging, he and his wife made us feel like members of an extended family. He was now in his fifties (which seemed ancient at the time), he was fit, lean and an avid rock climber. He would take his T.A.'s (which included me) to a spot at the far northern edge of the San Fernando Valley called "Stony Point." It was deemed to be the farthest southern point of glacier descent during some Ice Age or another, and had left great boulders for climbing clustered there. He would encourage and guide us up the rocks, constantly reminding us to "face your work." Stony Point always seemed like the middle of nowhere. 10 years later I would be living within a few miles of there, married and with two children.

The other "Al" was Alvin Smith. He was another T.A. and also a protege of Dr. Saxton. Very tall and skinny, he wore horn-rimmed glasses and had a pale complexion. He was also the only T.A. older than me—by almost 10 years. He had been a jazz drummer who played percussion and drove for an all female African American gospel singing group. They had opened for Bob Dylan a few times, and Alvin (he liked to be called Alvin, not Al) had lots of stories about being on the road with them during the 1960s. He'd gotten married, and his wife insisted that he leave the road and settle down. Alvin and his wife had split, but he remained in school—at least for a while. We quickly became close friends.

The other political people were mostly from the Latin American Studies Program. Many of them had ties to revolutionary groups in Central and South America. All of my friends on the left had one thing in common—they were philosophically materialist in their outlook. They believed that only the material world is "real" and that control of the means of production is the key to social change. Religion, the arts and the life of the mind are "superstructure," the topping on the cake of economic life.

There was nothing about this analysis that rang true to me. My experience of the power of the arts, and especially music, told me that there was more. And, if these arts were merely superstructure, why did Churches excommunicate, states censor and business buy up musicians and artists to keep them still or in service? Beyond that, I did not believe that materialism explained the past or pointed the way to a better future. On the other hand, these materialists certainly provided the best critique of how things operated now, and I shared with them a healthy revulsion at the current power arrangements in the world, and a desire to do something about it. As long we didn't get involved in abstract political discussions we got along fine. Alvin in particular loved jazz, blues and getting high. He was funny and a keen observer of life. What was not to like? Still, I was keeping my mind and heart open to new ways of seeing the world and how to transform it.

SEND THE DOG

In the time since I came to California, Ruth and I had been in constant touch. We were together during part of the summers and during a couple of vacations as well. We wrote letters and talked on the telephone frequently. Now, she was finally coming to join me for good.

Ruth's plan was to spend a year establishing residency in California, so that she would be able to enter UCLA without having to pay out-of-state tuition. She also planned to learn Spanish at the institute established by renowned philosopher and social critic Ivan Illich in Cuernavaca, outside of Mexico City.

Ruth arrived at the end of August. We spent several weeks getting used to living together and establishing our household. We repainted the kitchen and also the front door, which she decided should be bright red. We also played on the beach a lot. She brought her dog, a large German Shepard named "Puppy," with us to swim. It was the year when Venice changed forever, and we played our small, unwitting role in that transition.

The beach in Venice was very wide. From the "boardwalk" to the sea shore was more than 100 yards. The gay community in Venice, which was just emerging as an entity, decided that the area north of Windward Ave should become a nude beach. They began taking their clothes off and sunbathing in the buff. We, and other heteros, joined them. The LAPD did not approve. They would drive their cars on the cement frontage and come down onto the beach to "raid" the nudies. By the time they crossed the sand, everyone had their bathing suits on again, and there was no one to arrest. One day a reporter for the *LA Times* came down and wrote a story about this scene, including a picture of Ruth (not naked). After the story ran, people started congregating to watch the dance between the naked people and the police. Soon after that, people starting making tee-shirts and bringing other items to sell to the people who had gathered to watch. Buskers joined them, including the great Ex Swami X, a stand-up improviser of amazing talent and The Red Elvises, a group of Russian musicians who are still playing their Eastern European Rock and Roll to this day. Venice never did become a nude beach, but it never was the same quiet town again.

Meanwhile, school was beginning. I can still picture one early fall day. I was lifting weights in the Men's Gym. My friend Richard had picked Ruth up at my house and we were meeting on campus. I looked out the window and saw them walking towards the gym. The late afternoon sunshine caught Ruth from a particular angle, putting the rest of the area into shade. I felt the love rising in me as it had the first time I saw her, and I was so happy to have her with me at long last. A week later she left for Cuernavaca. Two weeks after that I got a telegram: "Have fallen in love. Send the dog." I never saw her again.

For the next year, when I came home in the afternoon I would immediately look at the mail, waiting in vain for a letter saying she had made a mistake and wanted to come home. I was used to living without her physical presence, even though I yearned for it. What I no longer had was some-one to whom I was emotionally connected in a deep way. I appreciated my parents and loved them for who they were and what they had gone through, but we were not part of each others lives in an intimate way. I had friends and people I liked, but it was not the same as being part of CADRE, with people I considered comrades in a fight against injustice, war and social insanity. I had no comrades, no family and no lover. I was alone.

I had been living alone for a while. At first I had room-mates, as the bungalow had two bedrooms and it halved the expenses. When the last one moved out I realized that I could swing the whole $100 rent, make an office out of one room and a real bedroom out of the other, and not have to worry about someone else in the place. I had shared a room until I left for college and a house or apartment until I subleased Jerome Arnold's place in Old Town for three months in 1967. Then back to sharing until now. I loved living alone. There certainly were some lonely nights think-ing of Ruth, but I would have had them whatever my living arrangements. I realized that I had essentially been living alone all my conscious life. Now I was learning to accept and enjoy that state, even while understanding that it would change again sometime.

I did not live alone for long. Nikolai Ivanovitch Lobachevski was a black lab puppy. I named him after a favorite character from a song by Tom Leher about a pla-giarizing mathematician. I had never had a dog before and had always wanted one. I had him for a few months when he disappeared from my yard and, despite an intensive search, was never seen again—at least by me. But I was hooked—I needed to find another dog.

I went back to the pound, where I had found Nikki. This time I came home with a female mutt. She looked like she had some shepherd, but was smaller. It turned out she had more retriever. She could retrieve a stick for as long as I would throw it—even into the ocean, where she would go through the waves in order to get that stick and bring it back. I named her "Emma"--not after Jane Austin's character, but after the great Anarchist/feminist organizer of the early 20th century, Emma Goldman.

I had seen other dogs badger their people when they were going to feed them, and resolved that my dog would be well trained. I taught her to sit under the kitchen table while I prepared her food. I would say "Table, Emma" and she would immediately go under the table and sit patiently. Ultimately she began to simply associate "table" with food. If I needed to call her, I would yell "table" and she would come running. She was smart, independent and loyal. I would sometimes take her to UCLA with me on my motorcycle. She would sit in front of me on the gas tank as we cruised the Santa Monica and San Diego Freeways. When I began to teach, she would lie at my feet. I told the class that she was responsible for discipline, but I don't think anyone believed me. When I left her alone in the front yard of my bungalow, she would escape and go down to the beach to play. Then she would come home and be back in the yard before I arrived. I only knew about her escapades by the smell of seaweed that clung to her coat. When she had puppies, (I was a bit lax about canine birth control) every one in the neighborhood wanted one of her offspring, though it was clear that there were several fathers involved in the litter. I did get her fixed after that. She was a wonderful companion and lightened my life considerably, opening my heart in a way that only a good dog can do.

EVERYONE GETS AN A

I loved being a teaching assistant. My experience as an antiwar organizer and orator made standing in front of a classroom full of college students feel tame in comparison. It also helped that I was six years out of college, making me closer to being an adult than most of the other assistants. I loved talking about history—what happened, how and why. I did not lecture—that was for the professor. I asked questions, in the Socratic method, and tried to push students to think as deeply as possible about the events and the issues they illuminated. I had my own opinions and attitudes, but I encouraged them to develop their own ideas, and to articulate them to others.

I also made it clear that grades were not important to me. Everyone started with an "A" in my class. As long as they showed up and did the assignments, they would keep that grade. I did give one of the students a "C". The professor just remarked, "Wow—he must have really pissed you off ." He had hardly showed up and didn't complete the work, and probably should have failed, but I wasn't the one to do that.

Being a teaching assistant also gave me a chance to indulge a life-long fantasy of becoming a stand-up comedian. I had been the class clown in grammar school and had spent time under the desk and outside the room for my antics.

Now I was the teacher, and there was no one to stop me. I loved comedy of all sorts, but especially the stand-up political types. Dick Gregory was a long-time hero, as was Lenny Bruce. Both spoke truth to power and challenged the status quo through ridicule, sarcasm and a finely honed sense of absurdity. And both were willing to do so at great personal risk to themselves and their careers, as Pete Seeger had done in the world of music. As a teaching assistant I had the chance to follow in their footsteps, or at least to try out material in front of a captive audience.

One of the most interesting classes I assisted on was "The History of Racial Attitudes in the United States." The teacher was Al Saxon, and Alvin Smith and I were the T.A.'s. That meant three white men were in charge of a class on race and racism. This was bound to raise hackles and pose challenges for us all.

On the first day of class, after the lecture, I went to the room to meet the students who had signed up for my section. The place was packed. I presumed that my reputation for easy grading had preceded me, but there were way more students than could be accommodated. What was I going to do?

I looked around the room and said, "OK. I want all the black people to go to this corner. All the brown people in this corner, the yellow people over here and the white people over there" while pointing to the four corners of the room. The students looked at me like I might be crazy but, hey, I was the teacher and they did what I told them to do. I counted the number of people in each location.

"There is room in the class for all the black, brown and yellow people. We will have to draw lots to see which white people get in." "That's not fair," said one white voice. "Your first lesson in the history of Racial attitudes in the United States," was my reply. All the minority students smiled, and the white students pulled pieces of paper out of a bowl to see if they would stay in the section. There were still plenty of heated discussions and confrontations during class, but I had succeeded in winning a degree of trust from the students that allowed a deeper level of conversation to take place between us all. During the last session we called in an inter-racial couple who specialized in facilitating "encounter groups" around race. Fear and resentment were expressed, but there was also an enhanced understanding of the dynamics of race and racial attitudes among the members of the class.

For the final exam, Al Saxon allowed the T.A.'s to include one question of our own on the test. I posed the following:

"It is some time in the future, and there is no racial prejudice in our country. How did we get from here to there? No answers involving supernatural events (e.g., an invasion by aliens that unites humanity) allowed."

The answers fell into one of two categories: A race war that annihilated one of the groups, or total intermarriage that erased all distinctions. No one could imagine a future in which we developed the capacity to accept and appreciate our differences and live together in harmony. It was very disappointing, and it reinforced my feeling that a new way of seeing these issues and their solutions was necessary if real social transformation was going to happen.

THE BOYS WITH THE BALLS

When I came to UCLA the school was at the height of its domination of Man's College Basketball. Lewis Alcindor (later to become Kareem Abdul Jabbar) had already graduated. For a couple of years the team did not have a great center to build around, but still managed to keep winning. The year I arrived was Freshman year for Bill Walton (freshman could not play varsity in that era) who was destined to be the next great center in college basketball. The team just kept on winning, guided by the "Wizard of Westwood," the legendary coach John Wooden. Unlike most schools, the basketball players were the kings instead of the football squad.

Coach Wooden insisted that his players pay attention to their schoolwork. Sidney Wicks, the starting forward, was not able to enter UCLA as a freshman because of academic deficiencies. He graduated as an academic all-American with a degree in Sociology. Basketball players began showing up in my sections—I had a good reputation as a teacher and an easy grader. On the first day of class of my second year as a T.A. I was sitting in Royce Hall waiting for Dr. Saxon to begin his lecture. I felt a tap on my shoulder and turned my head to see who it was. What I saw was a knee. I kept looking up and up until I saw this grinning face and a shock of red hair. It was Bill Walton. He said "Hi…can I be in your section?" I said "Anyone can be in my section. Just register."

For those who only know Bill as a sportscaster, a player, and/or a #1 Deadhead, you should know that in 1973, when we met, he was one of the most controversial figures in America. For the past several years basketball had become dominated by African-American players—especially at the center position. The specter of Wilt Chamberlain and Lew Alcindor jamming basketballs into the hoop over outstretched white arms had resulted in a rule outlawing dunking in college basketball from 1967 to 1976—often referred to as the "Alcindor rule." To some people, Bill represented "The Great White Hope," even as boxers such as Rocky Marciano had been touted in that sport. A 7-foot-2 redhead from San Diego, he could not have been more white. Unfortunately for these people and their expectations of him, he was vociferously and vocally opposed to the War in Vietnam, and was a very visible figure at demonstrations. He was also becoming a vegetarian. In short, he was a great disappointment for those who were looking for a new American hero in the John Wayne mode. Bill told me that the post office had once delivered a letter to him that was addressed "You Commie, Los Angeles CA." It was, indeed, directed towards Bill.

Bill was certainly the "big man on campus," and everyone wanted a piece of him. Everyone was super nice to him, tried to please him and in general wanted to maximize their time in his reflected glory. I was seven years older and significantly more experienced, and he trusted me as a mentor as well as a friend. He found it funny that I insisted on splitting the check when we ate together. I also told him the truth when he asked me a question, rather than telling him, as others did, what they thought he wanted to hear, or what might ingratiate themselves with him. After taking my class, he wanted to sign up for my section the next quarter and I suggested that he enroll in Alvin's section instead, so that he might experience a somewhat different approach. Even Susan, his girlfriend (later his wife), decided that I could be trusted and had Bill's best interests at heart. I did, however, take advantage of Bill's access to better weed than I could get—no one is perfect.

We would sometimes drive down to Palm Springs. There is a canyon on the west side of town called "Tahquitz Canyon." Today it is managed and protected by the Agua Caliente tribe, but in those days it was open to anyone who walked across the quarter mile or so of desert between downtown Palm Springs and the canyon entrance. Once inside, there was a large pond fed by a stream of melting ice that descended very rapidly from Idlywild Mountain, a mile above the desert floor. It could be over 100 degrees on the banks with a water temperature 50 degrees lower. People came to party there and often made a mess of this beautiful and sacred spot.

One could, however, climb up the canyon from there. It was a somewhat difficult ascent, but far from impossible, with a series of pools on different levels. You would climb in the heat and then plunge into the melted snow of the pools. A few times we would drop LSD and make the ascent—perhaps not the most brilliant of strategies, but it did seem like a good idea at the time. On one of these ascents we encountered a tribe member who lived in a cave near a pool. All the tribe members received an income based on the fact that Palm Springs is built on Native American land. This fellow, around our age, would come down from the mountain several times a year, cash a check and fly to San Francisco or some other nice destination for several weeks and then return to his cave on the Holy Mountain. We also met Vietnam Vets hiding out from the insane world below. But all of these people on the higher levels of the canyon understood the sacred element of the space and treated it with respect. They also recognized that those who made the climb shared their feelings about this holy spot.

There were many parties with the basketball team, especially after the season was over. At one gathering, just before the beginning of my last quarter as a T.A., the players started talking about a letter they had received from a girl who wanted to interview the whole team in order to "get to know the players underneath the uniform." Her name, they said, was "Randee Fling," and they took this letter and her name to be an invitation to "take on" the whole team. Such requests were not that unusual, although they were more often directed towards one or another of the star players, rather than towards them all. They were anxious to meet the writer and see if she was prepared to fulfill the promise they read into her letter.

The class I was to assist in my last quarter was called "History of Relationships between Men and Women in American History." The teacher was a woman, but both of her T.A.'s were men, which she was not happy about. Still, she was somewhat junior as a faculty member and did not have a choice in the matter. After the first lecture, I stood up to read the names of the people who had signed up for my sections. One of them was a morning section and the other was to meet at my house in Venice in the evening. As I read off the names, I came to one that was "Randee Flug." I read it out loud as Randee Fling. In the midst of the chaos a young woman approached me and asked "My name is Randee Flug, is that who you meant?" I hardly looked at her and said "Fling, Flug, what's the difference?"

HOW I MET YOUR MOTHER

The section I hosted at my home in the evening was full of students who had been in prior classes of mine, and many were friends. They included Greg Lee, one of the the starting guards on the basketball team. At six foot three, he was extremely handsome and the subject of crushes by many if not most of the girls on campus. He was very bright and articulate—an all-around heart throb. He was also, I knew, planning to ask this girl Randee about her letter—out loud and in public at the class. I was concerned, as I really did not want him to embarrass this poor young girl in front of everyone, and I was ready to step in and stop the conversation. So, as we all sat around my living room before class, Greg called out to Randee across the room to get her attention. She did not respond, so he called out again.

As it happened, she was talking to another girl when he spoke to her. She turned toward him, her long curly hair sticking out from her face, and replied, in a thick New York accent, "Are you talking to me? Can't you see I'm talking to her? Or doesn't it matter, since she's a woman?"

There was dead silence in the room. No one, certainly no female, had ever spoken to Greg like that. He was smart enough to realize whatever he had thought about "Randee

Fling" and her letter was not the case. I, on the other hand, said to myself "Wow, if this lady is for real, I need to meet her."

I had met and gone out with a number of women during my time at UCLA. Many of them called themselves "feminists" and were often members of feminist organizations on campus. They were conscious of the obstacles facing women in academia and in the larger society and were determined to scale these obstacles and find their place in the current system based upon their abilities. I understood and supported that goal, but I was interested in social transformation and in finding and knowing people who felt the same way. What is called "identity politics," that is, fighting for things that affect a certain group of people, has its place, but in the end it is a question of whether this fight leads to empathy with all others who are suffering, or whether one stops fighting when the immediate objective is won. In Randee's reply to Greg, I sensed a person of strength, courage and commitment. Within a few weeks we were living together, and have been ever since.

During one of our early conversations, which were at a speed and intensity that only people from New York can achieve, I heard the real story of the infamous letter. Randee had a contact at the New York Times. She had pitched a story to him about UCLA and the student fixation on basketball instead of politics. She wanted to include quotes from some of the other players, not just Bill, who was usually the only one the media cared about. Her reference to "the players beneath the uniforms" was the title of an article in Sports Illustrated about student athletes, in which Bill had complained about his teammates being ignored. As for her name, she had been thinking about changing it to "Rachael" as it sounded more mature and made clear she was a female. She soon did this, and has been "Rachael Flug" ever since. When we got married, people asked why we had two different last names. "Because I didn't want to change mine," was my standard reply.

Greg did not know any of these details, but he was smart enough to realize that the players' impression of "Randee Fling" was completely wrong. The day after the class, one of them called her on the dorm phone. All of the girls on the floor were amazed that someone on the basketball team was calling her. He wanted to know if they could still do the interviews. "Too late. The season is over and the Times has moved on."

The confusion over her name (the Randee part, not the Fling/Flug) had created some funny incidents in her career. She had been elected President of her high school in Massapequa, Long Island/New York. The county traditionally had the presidents of the high schools take over county offices for a day each year. The letter came to the school saying Randee would be the sheriff on this occasion. The student sheriff was always a boy, and when she and the deputy sheriff, who was a boy, arrived at the office, the sheriff laughed and suggested that they switch places. Randee had just looked at him and said "sure, if you want a visit from the ACLU." The deputy, who knew her, said he was very happy to be deputy, and Nassau County had their first female sheriff. She asked for a tour of the cells, spoke to inmates about their conditions and so on. The sheriff said it was the most interesting civics day of his career, and the incident was written up in Newsday, then a Long Island based newspaper.

Even though she was not yet nineteen when we met, Randee already had an extensive and impressive political resume.

She had organized a successful campaign ending the prohibition of girls wearing pants to school (in the New York winter!), taken on the school board when they tried to cut out driver's education and other student services, and organized marches against the war in Vietnam. She had interned for a New York State Supreme Court Justice (the first high school student to ever do that) and had organized high school students to work on behalf of Allard Lowenstein, the first congressman to be elected on an antiwar platform. His district had been gerrymandered to include Massapequa, which was far more conservative than the area taken out by the Republican State Legislature. She and her high school volunteers exceeded expectations in garnering votes in Massapequa, but Al still lost in a close election.

Al was a friend and mentor to many people in the progressive wing of the Democratic party. After his loss, a tribute dinner was held in his honor and Randee was asked to speak, along with John Tunney, the senator from California and other luminaries. When she and two of her young volunteers arrived at the dinner, they were seated way in the back of the hall, in the cheap seats. One the way to the table she heard people discussing the program. "Who is this Randee Flug"? "I think he's a black congressman from California," was the reply.

It was a long walk to the stage, through a quiet hall full of people wondering who this was. This young, unknown girl gave a speech that was reprinted in its entirety in the newspapers the next day. She received a standing ovation and, when she stepped down, she was invited to join one or another of the tables close to the front. Being who she was, she returned to her friends in their back corner. Her father carried the story from the papers in his wallet until it disintegrated. There was no question in his mind, or in the minds of many who knew her, that she would be the first woman senator from New York.

By this time Randee was a senior in high school and applying to colleges. She was planning to become a lawyer, but first there was undergraduate work to be done. She was accepted at Yale and Cornell among others, and was leaning towards Yale. Meanwhile, her parents were planning a move to California, which they had wanted to do for several years. Randee's older brother was graduating from Columbia and she was graduating from high school. It was the right time for them to make the big move.

Her father wanted her to go with them. He argued that it was foolish to spend all this money on Yale since she would still get into any law school she wanted to go to. Rachael (let me call her Rachael from now on) did not want to leave the East Coast and was adamant in her desire to go to Yale. Rachael's mom was not in the habit of defying her husband on matters of money, but she was supportive of her daughter's choice of schools.

Rachael had inherited some money from her mother's aunt. It was in trust for her until she was twenty-one. In those days, when one opened a bank account, the bank would gift a toaster or some other small appliance to the account holder. Because there was already an account in her father's name, they opened an account for this money under Shirley's (her mom) name to get the gift. Shirley wanted to let Rachael use the money from this account for school, and her father threatened divorce if she did so. She overheard this argument, and the next day announced that she had changed her mind and wanted to go to sunny California. She never let on that she had done so in order to save the marriage. It wasn't until much later that she realized the argument really wasn't about money. Going to UCLA would mean that her parents would pay out of state tuition for her for two years, which would have cost more than Yale on scholarship would have. Her father would not go on a plane, and he was afraid that if she stayed on the East Coast for school she would make her life there, and he would never see her again. He couldn't say that, so he made it about money instead.

When she got to UCLA she hated it. No one stayed up all night talking politics. Instead, they got up early, went to class and then the beach or some other outdoor activity. She applied for a position as a student lobbyist in Sacramento, and became the first first-year student to get the job. Her second quarter she was gone to the State Capitol.

Student lobbyists were supposed to represent the interests of the students to the legislators, something she had a great deal of experience doing through her high school political work. She quickly realized that her fellow lobbyists were there to make connections for themselves and advance their individual careers. One day, while walking through the Capitol building with a group of them, Rachael saw someone she knew from the Lowenstein campaign. Many college students had volunteered with Al. Most were from Yale, where Al had gone to Law School, or from Harvard, but one was from Stanford, where Al had taught. All the Yalees kind of made fun of him, with his cowboy boots and California drawl. Now Rachael saw him walking with the Speaker of the House and other government bigwigs. They hugged and kissed and began talking. Rachael asked him what he was doing there. He explained that while his name, Doug Chandler, meant nothing to the boys from Yale, his family owned, among other things, The Los Angeles Times and other media outlets in the state.

Her fellow student lobbyists were amazed that she was "friends" with Doug Chandler and expected that she would exploit this connection as they would have. Of course she did not, and soon she resigned from the lobby and returned to UCLA. Her plan was to finish the year and then transfer to Berkeley, where, she hoped, the student body would be more politically engaged than in Southern California.

Rachael had always had an interest in photography. Now, with time on her hands waiting for the quarter to end, she began taking pictures around campus. This included pictures of the basketball team at practices, which made a great subject for action photography. A girl who had been in a class with her saw her taking a picture of Greg Lee. The girl, of course, had a huge crush on Greg and approached Rachael about getting this picture from her. They began talking and Rachael told her about her plan to transfer to Berkeley. The girl, whose name was Varda, had been in a section I taught. She told Rachael that she should take a class from me before she left. "You'll love this guy," she told her.

That is what had brought Rachael to my class, even though she would normally never have chosen to be in a section run by a man. It also helped her overlook my idiot "Fling-Flug" remark and show up at the first class meeting. And that, children, is how the fates arranged for your mother and I to find each other.

MEET THE PARENTS

It was in the Spring of 1973 when I met Rachael. We began to spend almost all of our time together. She was officially living in a dorm, but was soon spending every night at my house in Venice. We had met while Emma the dog was pregnant. The first night Rachael was going to stay over I put Emma in the back yard so that we would not be disturbed. Rachael quickly set me straight on how pregnant creatures should be treated. She and Emma formed an immediate and irrevocable bond, and Emma stayed inside with us—although we did close the bedroom door that first night.

We talked passionately and incessantly about life, politics, people, art, and everything else. Even though she was not yet nineteen when we met, all my friends immediately recognized her fierce intelligence and commitment to her ideals. It also became evident that she was warm, compassionate and often very funny, with that caustic New York edge that set her apart from girls of California. Everyone recognized that we were a genuine couple, and that this whirlwind romance was becoming a life partnership.

That summer I was going back to Chicago to work for my father again. She was going back to New York for awhile. At this point she was still very much a New York Chauvinist, missing everything from pizza to politics back in the Big

Apple. I arranged a drive-away and we headed back east. I got us completely lost on a hike in Rocky Mountain National Park. She revealed a side of herself I had never seen when a lightning storm in Nebraska frightened her into hiding under the covers in the motel we were forced to stop at. We made it to Chicago, where my parents promptly fell in love with her. I found her a ride to New York and my father insisted on meeting the driver, seeing his license and taking down all his information before reluctantly agreeing that it was OK for her to go with him.

We said goodbye and that we would see each other back in Venice in the Fall. A week later the telephone rang. It was Rachael asking if she could join me in Chicago. I said of course. She arrived the next day. She said that New York was not her home anymore, and she was ready to commit to California.

When we got back, she and her friend Kathy found an apartment a few blocks away from my house in Venice. Susan, Bill's girlfriend and future wife, moved in with them. Even though Rachael was staying with me most of the time and Susan was with Bill, everyone wanted their own space as a backup.

At this point it is time to introduce Rachael's parents, Irv and Shirley. Irv was a CPA. He had been the controller at a local catering company on Long Island and had a small ownership share. The company was bought by a larger one, and his share of the buyout was what allowed them to move to California and for him to work part time, taking summers off to travel and go to Las Vegas, as he loved to gamble. He had been born in the Bronx and had served in World War II.

Shirley had been born in a small village in Poland. At the age of 9, in 1935, she was sent to the United States to live with her mother's sister, who had emigrated earlier and was married to a wealthy man in New York. Her aunt came to get her, but the Polish authorities would not allow Shirley to go on the U.S. ship with her aunt. She had to travel on a Polish vessel—even though her aunt was willing to purchase a ticket on the Polish ship and not use it. She made the passage herself, in the care of a kindly couple who watched over her. Later, her aunt brought Shirley's father over, to get established before the others joined them. But by then it was too late, and the rest of the family did not survive World War II. Her aunt always regretted not bringing her sister over first, but at the time people in the U.S. did not see the extent to which the Jews of Central Europe were in danger. Shirley said that her mother had asked the village Rabbi whether she should send her young daughter across the ocean alone and he said "Send her...you will save her life." Shirley told us that she had never felt afraid, that it had been a great adventure and she never regretted coming, although she missed her mother and sister very much. She remained with her aunt even after her father's arrival, and he made a new life for himself in the United States.

Her aunt's husband manufactured the cardboard inserts that went into low-end ladies pocketbooks or purses. His business thrived during the depression and Shirley went from the Shetel (the small, backward villages of Eastern Europe) to an elevator building in the nicest part of the Bronx. She quickly learned English and became an American girl.

Irv and Shirley had met before the war and became engaged before he went overseas. They married soon after his discharge, living with family in the Bronx. Irv wanted to be a salesman but lacked the temperament and social skills necessary for success. He was really good with numbers and got his degree from CCNY in accounting. Soon he became a CPA. Rachael's older brother, Glen, was born in 1950. When Rachael came along in 1954 Irv was doing well enough to move the family to Long Island, where the GI Bill helped them buy a home with a yard for $8,000 in the newly developed area of Massapequa. This had been farmland less than a decade before, but the farms were now subdivisions full of young children and their families. Ron Kovic, author of *Born on the Fourth of July*, and Jerry Seinfeld are two other Boomers from that town.

When Rachael and I met, her parents were living in an apartment in Santa Monica. They were never quite sure of what to do with their fiercely intelligent and independent daughter, who was not afraid to voice her opinion on any topic and also to act on her convictions in a fearless manner. When she was 12 she began studying for her Bat Mitzvah ceremony at the Synagogue in which both of her parents were very active. As her 13th birthday was approaching, she saw the boys being pulled out of class for one on one sessions to learn the readings from the Torah (the five books of Moses) that were part of the ceremony. She asked the teacher when she would begin this process. When he told her that only boys could read from the Torah, she walked out of the class and refused to be Bat Mitzvahed, even though there would be a big party and lots of presents. Her father didn't argue—he said it was the first time her principles would save him money. The people at the synagogue felt badly and wanted to call Rachael to the dais to give her a gift, but her father advised them that they would regret giving her a forum for talking.

I did not meet Rachael's parents for a while after we began seeing each other. Shortly after beginning UCLA, Rachael had been asked out on a date by an African-American student in her class. Rachael didn't date very much in high school, being far too busy with politics. She didn't wear makeup or dress for boys. So, when Rachael told her parents that she was going out with someone, they were very excited. When she told them he was black, they were very upset. The feeling of almost all Jewish parents was that you shouldn't date outside of your religion, because if you don't date you won't fall in love and you won't get married. You were just looking for trouble by beginning the process. This was twice as true across racial lines, at a time when inter-racial couples were rare and the subject of discrimination and scorn on both sides of the racial divide.

They did not want to meet this boy. Rachael told them that if they wouldn't meet him they wouldn't meet anyone she went out with. So, the first time I went to pick up Rachael at her folk's apartment, I rang the bell and went back to the car. Alvin and his girlfriend were with us. He said to me "Is that Rachael's parents at the window up there? Why are they looking at us with binoculars ?" I looked up and tipped my hat to them, as they quickly retreated into the room and closed the curtains. It was several weeks before we were introduced. In the meantime, Rachael's mom figured out that we must be more seriously involved. She called Rachael at the dorm fairly early one morning. Rachael's roommate tried to cover for her by saying she was at the library doing research, but Rachael's mom knew it was too early for her daughter to be up and about, and figured she must have slept over at my place.

When Rachael told her parents about her moving in with Kathy and Sue, they were aghast and suggested that she should "live with them" even if she was, in fact, staying at my house every night. Rachael couldn't be bothered with the pretense and refused. When they finally revealed this shameful secret to a friend back East she replied that her daughter was doing the same, and that all the kids were living in sin and thinking nothing of it. This made them feel better, but they still never let us stay together in their home before we were married, even when we were living out of town and came to visit. In those days, it was called "the generation gap."

SEPTEMBER 11, MARIO, AND THE FBI

The 1973–74 school year began early in September. I was no longer a teaching assistant but had to remain in school as I was still on probation. At this point I had my Master's degree and had finished my coursework for a PhD. All that remained were the oral and written exams and the writing of a PhD dissertation. In other words, all the work of graduate school, without any pay. Rachael, in the meantime, had her regular classes to attend to.

Very soon after school began an event occurred that fundamentally changed our lives. On September 11, 1973, the democratically elected government of Chile, headed by Socialist President Salvador Allende, was overthrown by the Chilean military in a bloody coup de tat directed and supported by the United States. Allende was killed, as was the Nobel Poet Pablo Neruda and Victor Jara, the beloved blind singer and guitar player whose hands were first cut off so that he could not play. Thousands of labor leaders and students were rounded up and driven to the soccer stadium in Santiago, where many were taken out and slaughtered, as were other "enemies of the regime" all over the country. A friend from the Latin American Studies department was in the country at the time and ended up in the Stadium. His US passport saved his life, and he came back to California shaken to the core by his experience. It was the inauguration of a brutal military dictatorship that lasted until 1988, aided and abetted all the while by the United States Government, which had no problem interfering with a democracy that had existed since 1932 when that democracy threatened American economic interests in the region. Henry Kissinger, who was about to win the Nobel Peace Prize for "helping to end the war in Vietnam" was the principal architect of the Chilean policy. The granting of the Peace Prize to him is generally accepted as the moment when satire and reality met, with satire as the loser. Tom Lehrer, the great musical satirist of the 1950's and '60's, quit writing songs after this and returned to his career as a math teacher, saying that there was nothing more absurd he could come up with. Years later my daughter had him as a teacher at UC Santa Cruz, where she was the only one in her class who knew of his former life.

The events in Chile were both tragic and revelatory. At first, Rachael and I talked about going to Chile and working with the Resistance there. Our friends in the Latin American Studies department, many of whom had connections to left wing groups in South and Central America, pointed out to us that two Gringos who did not speak Spanish and didn't know how to shoot a gun would be of negative value to any resistance movement in Chile. I thought of my uncle Bernie in Spain and reluctantly agreed with their assessment.

Rachael and I spent many hours talking about the coup and its implications. In January 1974 we got a phone call from our friend Richard White, who was one of those Latin American Studies graduate students with ties to the

Left in South America. He said that a friend of his had just returned from traveling in that area and needed a place to stay while he got settled. Could he stay with us? We replied, "Of course...any friend of yours is a friend of ours." We told him that we would not be home until late that evening and would leave the door unlocked for our guest. When we got home we found Mario Savio sitting on our futon couch.

We immediately recognized Mario. The Sicilian firebrand spokesperson for the Free Speech Movement was one of the originators of the "student rebellions" taking place all over the country. Clearly a towering intellect, he was also a passionate speaker who felt and could articulate the hypocrisies inherent in the positions held by those in authority, while maintaining a deep level of compassion for those suffering from the abuses of the rich and powerful. It was typical of Mario that, while seeking a place to stay, he specifically told Michael not to say who it was for. He wanted to stay with people who would give a place to "anyone" rather than someone who would love to have a celebrity like Mario as a guest. We became close friends and remained so for several years. Today, Mario would most likely be diagnosed as "bi-polar," with his mood swings from excitement to deep depression. I would say that he was enormously sensitive on both a personal and social level, a gentle soul who had no desire for the spotlight he had fallen into, but who believed in the righteousness of what had to be done and who refused to back down to authority in any form.

It was at this time that one of the most bizarre events of that bizarre time took place. On February 4, 1974, Patricia Hearst was kidnapped in Berkeley, CA. Her kidnappers were a heretofore unknown revolutionary group that called itself the "Symbionese Liberation Army," or SLA. No one knew what, if anything "Symbionese meant, but they kidnapped this member of the wealthy and influential Hearst family from her home in Berkeley, where she was an apolitical student at the University. There followed ransom requests for food giveaways and, ultimately, a bank robbery in which it appeared that Patricia was an active participant. She was indicted for her part in this robbery and declared herself an "active member" of the SLA.

The group fled San Francisco and came to Los Angeles, where local and federal law enforcement were trying desperately to find them. In the midst of this, the local Pacifica Radio Station asked Mario to be interviewed about this situation. In the course of the interview Mario answered a question in a way that could have been interpreted that he knew where they were hiding—which he did not. Still, when he got home from the interview, we got a call from Richard White pointing out this possibility. He told us that, within the next day or so, someone would come to our door in Venice saying they were taking a survey or looking for a gas leak. "Invite them in and let them look around. They will be the FBI looking for Patty Hearst and it is important that they don't think you are hiding anything."

We immediately moved our stash into the back yard and awaited their arrival.

The next day, while I was out doing something and Rachael was home alone, the knock came. She invited the "gas man" in, asked him to check every room and the attic crawl space as well. He did so, proclaimed the house safe, and left. It was our first encounter with the FBI around Patty

Hearst, but not our last. Mario, of course, was chagrined and apologetic about bringing this down on us, but we assured him that we were fine.

During all this time, our intense discussions of what a "revolution" meant and how it could happen continued unabated, with Mario joining us with his intensity and intellect. We would sometimes talk all night, deciding nothing but utterly engrossed in the conversation. After Mario found a place to live and moved out, Rachael and I continued talking about "what to do." We were both committed to social transformation and did not want to waste our time doing things that would not work. At the time, there was much discussion about working "within the system" or "outside the system." It seemed to us that the people of Chile had worked "within the system", democratically electing a socialist. The reaction of the "system", meaning those who actually held the reins of power, was to unleash the military and the national police upon them. This, along with a long history of people within the United States working for change and being co-opted, led us to the conclusion that "working from inside" was not a path we wished to follow.

At the same time, we also saw that the forces opposed to change had all the guns and all the money. The system itself was "guns and money" and if change had to be accomplished through these means, change would not happen. This was certainly in accordance with our belief in non-violence as both a means and an end in itself, since the society we wanted to see was one in which force and coercion were not used to control other human beings. If this was going to be possible, however, it was becoming clear to us that alternative sources of power had to be available to us, and that we had to be able to recognize and connect to these positive forces of the universe in order to overcome the negative ones. It was the beginning of our conscious search for the connection between "Spirituality and social change," a search and a way of working that has informed the rest of our lives.

ALDO AND JOHNNY

In the winter of 1974 the country was in a state of turmoil. The Watergate hearings were proceeding, with revelation following revelation that would lead to the ultimate resignation of President Nixon in August. The vice-president, Spiro Agnew, was being indicted for taking bribes while Mayor of Baltimore and Governor of Maryland. He also would resign, but a deal was made so that he would not spend a day in jail. In the meantime, my five years of probation were coming to an end. I still owed the government more than $2,000 of the $3,000 fine associated with my sentence. On March 21, 1974, I showed up at the Federal Building to meet with my probation officer. He immediately told me that they were going to violate me for failing to live up to my obligation and I would serve the full three years in jail.

I knew that my parents would front me the money for the fine, but I really didn't want their money to go to fund bombs any more than I wanted my own. So, I looked my probation officer right in the eyes and said "Let me get this straight. You are going to pull an A student out of graduate school because he can't pay a fine for a misdemeanor offense while the vice-president gets off with no jail time for taking bribes while in office. You can do this, but I guarantee that half of UCLA will be in front of this building tomorrow and every columnist in the country will have a field day at your expense."

He looked at me and said "Get out of here…but we'll see you again." So far he has been wrong, but hey, you never know. I left his office a free man again.

Several months before this I had gotten a call from Jordan, my old friend from Chicago. He was coming to town to be on a television quiz show. Did I want to come to the taping? "Of course," I replied. I went to the studio with his mother and watched him win some money and a new car. My immediate reaction was "If Jordan Epstein can do this, so can I." However, I needed to wait until I was off probation so none of the money could be claimed by the government. While waiting, I watched the show whenever I could. It was called "Split Second", and was based upon how much you knew and how quickly you could access the information. This was before the age of Trivial Pursuit, when people began trying to learn unimportant facts. I happened to have a lot of them in my head and found that when I played along with the contestants, I usually won. Of course, I had to get on the show, and long-haired hippies were not often seen on television—and never as contestants on game shows.

A few days after getting off probation, I went down for the tryout. I did very well on the test and in the game-playing portion of the interview. I had tied my hair up and trimmed my beard. They told all of us that they would call within three weeks if they wanted us to appear on the show. I went down to the parking garage, got into my Volkswagen Square-back with the hood missing, and went back to Venice. Soon after returning home, the phone rang. It was the production assistant calling to ask if I was available to be on the show next week. "Are kidding? Of course," was my reply. "Be here Monday morning at nine-and don't bother putting your hair up."

I later found out that the producers had left the office at the same time I did and saw me getting into my ragged old car.

"Wow, this guy really needs a new car. Let's put him on right away," was their reaction.

Rachael and I were fine with our old VW. Our plan was to sell whatever car I won and use the money to live on. The winner of the game got to choose among five cars. If the chosen one started when the winner turned the key, they got the car. If it did not, they came back to play on the next show. If they won again, one of the cars was eliminated and they got to choose among four cars, increasing their odds of winning. If they won five times, they would win whatever car was left. We researched the cars and I would always choose the car I could sell for the most money.

Five shows were filmed in one day—two in the morning and three after lunch. I was on the first show. When the host, Tom Kennedy, introduced the contestants he asked what we did for a living. I didn't have a job and was leaving UCLA, so I improvised and said "I investigate corporate crime." "Oh, you mean like embezzlement?," he asked. "No, I mean like pollution. After all, it's our air, too!"

The audience applauded wildly.

I won the game, but it was very close. When Tom asked me which car I thought would start, I said "My girlfriend is in the audience. She has psychic ability so I'd like to ask her to choose." He asked her and she, sticking to the plan, picked the most expensive car, a Pontiac Le Mans station wagon. It didn't start, and Tom made a joke about her intuition.

When he introduced the contestants for the next show he said "This is our champion, Abraham Entin."

Then, instead of asking me any questions, which was the usual thing to do, he said "Now let's meet his challengers."

I won that game as well, but the Pontiac still did not start. The same thing happened when I was introduced on the third show. It was clear they were not going to give me a chance to make any more anti-corporate remarks on the air.

Both games had been close. By the third game I hit my stride, and racked up way more points than either of the other two contestants. I needed just one answer on the final round to go for the car again. Three pairs of first names showed up on the board. One of the pairs was "Aldo and Johnny."

Before Tom could read the question I buzzed in and said "The answer is Ray; it's Aldo and Johnny Ray." He looked down quizzically at his answer sheet. "He's right-the question is what last name to these people share—It's Aldo and Johnny Ray!"

This time the Pontiac started. When Tom leaned into the car to congratulate me he said "I'm sure you'll do something good with the money." I figured that the producers had realized I would always go for this car and wanted to get me off the show, so they made sure it would start this time. I had won about $2000 in cash plus the car. I was richer than I had ever been. Later that night, when we were celebrating, Rachael told me that she did know which car would start when I asked for her help. The curtain had blown open a little while the stagehand was setting the car and she had seen which one he was working on.

"Didn't you see how close that game was? How could you not tell me which one would start?"

"We had a good plan-besides, I knew that you would win the car eventually."

I never doubted her psychic abilities again.

GETTING OFF THAT LA FREEWAY

There was nothing to keep me in school any longer. But what about Rachael and her plans to be a lawyer? Since Rachael's parents did not want to subsidize her decision to live with me, she had taken a part time job at a department store in Century City, seven miles from our place in Venice. She did not have a car, and the Los Angeles public transportation system had not improved since my experience trying to get to the taxi garage. So, she often hitchhiked to work. Hitch-hiking was legal, as long as one stayed on the curb and did not stand in the street itself. One day, as she was standing on the sidewalk of Lincoln Blvd, the main drag through Venice, trying to get a ride to work, a motorcycle cop stopped and gave her a ticket for hitch-hiking. She pointed out to him that she was on the sidewalk, but he said that "girls should not be hitch-hiking, and he was giving her the ticket for her own good." Of course, she went to court.

She prepared a chart showing where she was standing and planned her cross examination, etc. When the day came, I dropped her off at the West Los Angeles traffic court building and continued on to UCLA to do some things while she was in court, having spent enough time in traffic courts over the years. When I came back she was sitting on the steps of the courthouse. Everyone who came out from the building stopped to say how happy they were to have been in court to see the show.

She explained to me that the cop had not lied on the stand—he agreed that she was standing on the sidewalk. When she asked him his position on girls hitch-hiking, the judge disallowed the question as irrelevant. Rachael objected and he overruled her objection, at which point she registered her exception to his decision. Ultimately, the judge said he would void her fine but rule against her. She said "you think I did this for the money? I don't care about the fine, I care about justice." He threatened to hold her in contempt, she dared him to, and he finally had his two very large bailiffs pick her up by her arms and carry her out of the courtroom while she kicked and screamed. It was the most exciting thing to happen in traffic court in years, and I was, and remain, so sorry to have missed it. Still, for Rachael, it raised questions about what could be accomplished through the legal system, and it reminded her of a comment made by the judge for whom she had clerked during high school. He had told her then that she was too interested in justice to ever function in the legal system. She didn't know what he meant at the time, but was beginning to understand it now.

I told her the story of my friend Paul, a classmate at the University of Chicago. Paul's father and older brother were both lawyers, and there was an expectation that he would go the same route. He did, but without the same enthusiasm— except for the continued deferment from the Army, which proved motivation enough to get through. After graduation he moved to Berkeley and set up practice. His first client was a mutual friend of ours who had also moved west from

Chicago. He was a black man from the South Side named Louis, who had hung around the University. He was smart and funny and a good friend. He was certainly smart enough to leave Chicago and go to California.

Louis had bought a bicycle from someone and then realized that there was a chance the seller had stolen the bike he had bought. So, Louis took the bike down to the police station to check out its status. He was correct—the bike had been stolen, and the police promptly arrested him for receiving stolen goods. He called Paul for help.

The whole thing was outrageous. If he were white, the cops would have given him a good citizenship award for bringing the bike in. Instead, they arrested him.

As a person, Paul wanted to lambast the whole system for its racism and injustice. As a lawyer, he had to advise Louis to hold his head down and do the "yassa boss shuffle," rather than coming off as an angry black man with a good reason for being angry. Louis took his advice and got off with a warning. Paul became a Volkswagen mechanic and never practiced law again.

The question facing Rachael was whether or not she was willing and able to deal in the compromised and compromising legal system, or if there was a better way for her to work on the changes she wished to see in the world.

It had been more than six months since the coup in Chile, and the dictatorship was solidifying its hold on the country. Chancellor Young, the head of UCLA, had issued an invitation to the Junta to come up to Campus so that the University might help them with their work. This was the final straw. Rachael had no desire to continue in school. The question became, where would we go from here?

Bill's career at UCLA was also coming to an end. The season was over and the upcoming NBA draft would certainly find him the number one draft pick—with a contract to match. Bill and Susan asked Rachael and I to take a ride with them up to Paso Robles, a small town about two hours north of Los Angeles, just off the 101 Highway. It was a very warm and sunny place, about ten miles inland and just north of Santa Barbara. There was a ranch property for sale there. Bill wanted to buy it. It had two houses, a main house and a small place near the gate. It was a very beautiful property, and they proposed that Rachael and I live rent-free in the gate house and continue our political work from there. They would live in the main house, and if Susan wanted to stay at home during the season while Bill was traveling and concentrating on basketball, we would be there for her. It sounded ideal, and we agreed. We would let our great bungalow in Venice go, and move up the road a piece.

For quite a while I had allowed the Venice food co-op to use my garage to store food. When they moved out I had allowed Becky's (our next door neighbor) sister's boyfriend to use the garage to fix cars, in exchange for taking care of my old Volkswagen square-back (the one without the hood). We told them they could have the house when we moved out. Everyone was thrilled.

The NBA draft happened, and Bill was chosen by the Portland Trailblazers. Bill had not hired a lawyer or agent to represent him in the contract negotiations. Instead, he had allowed the "godfather of UCLA Basketball," Sam Gilbert, to negotiate for him. A very bad idea. It turned out that Bill did not get enough to buy the property, which was all he really wanted. He believed that Sam had sold him out, and was working with the NBA owners to help deliver UCLA players for less than it would cost them otherwise. There was no question that Sam had a shadow side—he was later indicted for a money laundering scheme—and committed many violations of NCAA rules in his time as a "fixer" for the program, which also received a two year suspension for his activities. Whether or not he actively sold Bill out, it was the end of their long relationship and the end of Bill's dream ranch.

We did not actually hear the news about the ranch directly from Bill. We didn't hear anything for a while, and it was only a week or two before we were to vacate our place in Venice when we found out we had no place to go. We knew we could turn around and tell Becky's sister that the deal was off, but we decided that it was time for us to take a step into the unknown. We had the money from Split Second plus the small inheritance Rachael had from the aunt who had raised her mother. We would get into the old squareback and leave. Santa Barbara was the obvious place to start our new life.

Rachael's parents could not believe she was leaving school and all the dreams of a political career. They knew that I had not convinced Rachael to do this, but they still associated me with the decision. Her mother could see that we loved each other and that made it easier for her. It took her father a lot longer to accept the new reality of his daughter's life.

WAITING FOR EVERYMAN

Why Santa Barbara? Aside from the fact that it was close, beautiful and had perfect weather? We knew someone there who was enmeshed in the spiritual supermarket that was Santa Barbara in 1974. His name was Hank Babcock. Bill Walton had introduced us to him a few months earlier. Hank had been a highly recruited guard in the Los Angeles High School private school league who had chosen UCLA for college. After playing on the freshman team he decided to drop out of basketball and college to immerse himself in a quest for spiritual enlightenment.

Hank resembled Greg Lee—both were tall, white and handsome. Hank's hair was lighter, his features softer, and he was trying to develop an aura of gentleness and humility. He lived in a small room in a house with several other spiritual seekers, and knew seemingly everyone in the large and diverse spiritual community. He introduced us to a psychic astrologer who told me that I had had a harem in one past life and had been beheaded because of things I had said in another. Both made perfect sense to me. He introduced us to Indian Holy men and indigenous spirit healers. We also met people from The Sunburst Community, who owned and operated a number of organic stores, bakeries and restaurants in the Santa Barbara area.

Many people know of Sunburst (if not by name) through Jackson Browne's classic song, "Everyman," in which he says "Everybody I know is waiting to leave by the light of the morning"... On a live recording he talks about knowing these people who not only wanted to leave, but had the boat ready to sail away. That was Sunburst. They owned land in the mountains above the town and lived there while they earned enough money through the farm and stores to finance their voyage, which was to be made on a 158ft sailing vessel they owned. They never did leave, but at one time they were the largest purveyor of natural foods in the U.S.

We tried to find a place to live around town. We came across an ad for a place owned by a Santa Barbara resident, but which was located in the Kern River Canyon East of Bakersfield, CA. It was a cabin right on the river, where the air was hot but the water cold. We decided that we would rent the place for the summer and then figure out what our next step would be.

The Kern River begins in the Sierra Nevadas and ends outside of Bakersfield, where its waters are diverted for irrigation and other uses. Lake Isabella, an Army Corps of Engineers-created body of water, divides the Upper and Lower Kern River, and white water rafting is very popular on both sections of the Kern. The lower Kern is especially dangerous for swimming, with swift currents prevalent down the center of the river.

When we there in the summer of 1974, the canyon was accessible only via a two lane winding road on the south side of the river. A new, straight, four lane highway was being built on the north side, in order to facilitate development in the area. The men working on the road were very happy to see these naked hippies in the river below and, when there was blasting scheduled, drew lots (we found out) to see who would go over and warn us about the upcoming noise.

The cabin was pretty much a shambles, and it was really too hot to even sleep inside. We dragged the mattress outside and slept under the stars. Rachael was not a morning person, but I was always able to rouse her by pointing out the red ants that were waking up and about to feast on us at sunrise. At night I would read *Childhood's End*, Arthur C. Clark's science fiction classic, out loud, and we would gaze at the incredible array of cosmic phenomena in the desert sky. There was also the morning when we awoke to see Emma sniffing curiously at a very large rattlesnake, who was coiled and ready to strike at her. Rachael let out a blood-curdling scream. The rattler ran one way, Emma ran another, and I froze in horror, not having the slightest notion of how to respond to the situation. Nothing in Brooklyn, Chicago or Los Angeles had prepared me for this kind of outdoor experience.

We stayed at our hideaway all summer, with occasional trips into Bakersfield for provisions. The cabin was below the road and we left our car up above, near the mailbox. One day, about a month after we had arrived, we went up to check the mail. There was a note in the box that said a letter was waiting for us at the post office in town. Since we needed some supplies, we put on clothes for a change and went into town to pick up the letter and groceries. When we got to the post office, all the employees came out when we showed up. It turned out that the letter was from Bill Walton, and everyone wanted to see who he was writing to, which was why they had not left the letter in our mailbox.

The letter invited us to come to Portland, where Bill was beginning his pro career as a member of the Portland Trailblazers. Rachael and I talked it over during the weeks before our rental was up. We did not want or expect to live with Bill and Susan, and would not have gone just to join them. We did not want our lives and destiny tied to theirs. On the other hand, both Jordan (who had introduced me to Split Second) and Emily (who I had lived with during the DNC in Chicago) were both there. I had visited them on my move from Chicago to LA, and it seemed like an interesting place where the air would be cleaner than Los Angeles and rentals cheaper than Santa Barbara. We decided to go.

PART IV

FINDING THE PATH

THE PUSHERS OF CANCER

When we arrived in Portland, a little after Labor Day of 1974, it was raining. It didn't stop until Memorial Day of 1975. When it did, people told us it had been a light year for rain.

The weather was perfect for us. The cold and dark were conducive to staying home, reading, researching and, later, writing. Having grown up in chillier parts of the country, the rain did not stop us from going out when we wanted or needed to. Compared to Chicago, the downpours of Portland felt like spring showers. At least it wasn't snowing. One night it did snow—about ¼ of an inch. We went out to an event and were stunned that it had been canceled because of the "snow storm." This was not Chicago—or New York.

We were going to stay with Bill and Susan in their new house in Lake Oswago, a new, upscale section of town South of the City. The house had been custom built for Bill, and fit his dimensions. It was a dream house for someone his size. The problem was that he did not do much food prep, and a normal-sized person needed a step-stool to reach the kitchen counters. It was also disconcerting to sit on the toilet with your feet dangling above the floor. Still, it was a lovely home.

When we arrived, no one was there, but the door was open. We came in and looked around. There was a book sitting on the dining room table. It was entitled *The Mucous-less Diet*. We opened it to a chapter that described the effects of ingesting decaying animal carcasses, otherwise known as meat, on the human digestive system. We had already been leaning towards a plant-based diet, and reading this sealed the deal.

This was typical of our time in Portland. We had sep-arated ourselves from the University and all the socially sanctioned viewpoints and approaches we had been taught. "Question authority" was the dictum we were living by. We were committed to trying out any and all new ideas and viewpoints that came our way, submitting them to the test of our own intelligence and feel for the truth. This led us into some strange highways and byways, from Pantheism to the Essenes on the spiritual side, to the Bilderburg Group and the Masonic Order on the political. The strangest of these byways was the "Hollow Earth," which we came across in a book of that title. It posited a race of beings living at the core of the planet and affecting human life from that vantage point. This was leading us to a new ice age. We went down to the Army Surplus store to get some Korean War hats—the kind they wore on Mash—and other cold weather gear. After trying them on we looked at each other, shook our heads and put the stuff back. We decided that if it was going to become that cold, we would freeze with the rest of the population.

Our newly kindled interest in diet and health led us deep into the phenomenon of addiction. We came to the real-ization that the American way of medicine and health was focused on curing illness, rather than building health. This made perfect sense. A big part of being healthy comes from consuming less. "I can't believe I ate the whole thing" was a very successful ad campaign for Alka Seltzer. "Eat it all-then take a pill" is much better for the economy than abstention. Suddenly, all around us we could see the urge towards mindless consumption being cultivated among the American people. We would drive around Portland at night taking photos of billboards that said "You can't eat just one" and other messages telling us to consume our way to happiness.

In 1974–75, the word *addiction* was all about heroin. The image of the addict was a junkie with a needle in his arm. Even alcoholics were not considered "addicts" in the same way. Today we have support groups and whole sections of bookstores aimed at helping people with all manners of substance and behavioral addictions, from chocolate to gambling to sex. But, for us at that time, the idea that we were deliberately being addicted to an unhealthy way of eating and living was a revelation that blew our minds. It was a earthquake of consciousness rivaling and re-enforcing what I had experienced more than twenty years before, under my desk during the "duck and cover" exercises of the first and second grade. But now we understood that it wasn't that they didn't know, but that we were being deliberately deceived about the most fundamental issues of health and wellbeing.

Today, very few people are shocked to find out that the tobacco industry knew of the links between smoking and cancer for decades and routinely suppressed the information, while maintaining there was no "scientific evidence" showing this to be the case. Or that the fossil fuel industry knew the reality of climate disruption and the role of their business model in this ongoing disaster. But this was only forty years ago, and even we, who considered ourselves to be political sophisticates, were truly shaken to discover that everything we were being fed was a lie. Our parents, who we knew loved us and wanted the best for us, had fed us formula instead of breast feeding, because the "experts" told them it was better for us. We were raised on Wonder Bread, that "built strong bodies eight ways" and given Twinkies as treats and rewards.

As we followed this thread we saw that refined sugar was in everything from baby formula to medicines. We began to roam the aisles of supermarkets, obsessively reading labels. In all my years of delivering Stella D'oro biscuits and cookies I had never read the ingredients listed on the packages. When I did, my stomach turned. They were full not only of sugar (they were, after all, cookies) but of artificial colors and flavors, preservatives and other unpronounceable ingredients. They were no better and no worse than anything else we found on the shelves.

On a personal level, all of this led us to a more and more simple diet. We went all the way to Fruititarianism, living on bananas, oranges and apples. We bought a kit for a food dehydrator, which Jordan helped us put together, and began buying overripe bananas by the case at the central market and making leather out of them. After a little while, we realized that eating all this fruit in the Portland winter was not the best diet possible, and switched to whole grains and vegetables. We found a great soup and bread restaurant near downtown, run by a spiritual group. When we shared Thanksgiving with Jordan and his family, we pigged out on a giant yam.

At some point during this period we came across a pamphlet created jointly by the Food and Drug Administration (FDA), the American Medical Association (AMA) and the

American Cancer Society (ACS). This was our government, the leadership of the scientific community and the largest non-profit advocate for cancer patients and research. The name of the pamphlet was "How to Recognize a Cancer Quack." It listed ten ways to spot these charlatans who were looking to dupe us and take our money while ped-dling their false remedies. The number one sign was that they told us there was a connection between diet and can-cer. If your doctor told you this, you should immediately report them to the proper authorities for investigation so that they might have their license revoked and, most prob-ably, face criminal prosecution.

We knew, of course, that there were charlatans and "snake oil salesmen" out there, ready to pick the pockets of the desperate and and unwary. But this was the leadership in government, science and philanthropy saying that anyone who disagreed with them on a matter of basic medial sci-ence was automatically a criminal. We knew that many of the people saying this sincerely believed it and thought they were protecting us. But we also knew there were those in responsible positions who knew that this was a lie and who fed it to us anyway. We were following Jefferson Airplane down the rabbit hole where "the truth is found to be lies" and "the pills that mother gives you don't do anything at all," becoming pawns in the games played between the white and red queens of the world. Once again we were approaching the place where politics and metaphysics meet, and the fun-damental question of good and evil and how they work in our world was staring us in the face. Some of these authori-ties may have been stupid, but at its core, the system was evil manifesting in the world.

All of this culminated in a feverish few weeks of writing which produced our first published work—a pamphlet entitled *The Pushers of Cancer.* It traced our lives from baby food to sugar-coated cereals to fast foods, to acne and cosmetics—all the way to cancer, and the promise of a cure that will allow us to continue living the way we do, and never suffer the consequences. The cover featured a well-known brand baby with a syringe in its head. The syringe had "taste is everything" written down its glass tubing. It was a powerful and scary piece of work.

We found an old mimeograph machine at a garage sale and moved it into the basement of our house. We began emulating the radicals of old, turning out their incendiary leaflets in the tenements of cities around the world. We took *The Pushers* everywhere we could think of, and sent it to everyone we knew. Because we had also talked about the ban on any alternative to "cut, nuke and burn" as treatments for cancer, we sent a copy to the International Association of Cancer Victims and Friends. They loved the pamphlet and wanted to buy a few hundred copies. We quickly contacted an old CADRE comrade who had become a "movement printer" in upstate New York. He printed them for us on better quality paper, with the cover I described, and we sent the Association their copies, with several hundred left for us to distribute elsewhere.

We also established the "If you feel you heal Research Association" as a vehicle for promoting our work. The name came from a Robert Downey Sr. film entitled "Greasers Palace," which featured Jesus returning to Earth in a Zoot suit and healing people by laying on hands and reciting the mantra *If you feel, you heal.* Our logo was the picture of the truth seeker from the Tarot deck, holding his lantern in the darkness. We sent our brochure out to many groups, looking for opportunities to speak about these issues. We did get some responses, but events overtook us before we could follow up on these inquires. Still, this episode reinforced our quest to find the source of positive spiritual energy needed to transform the world.

THE KUNG FU KIDS

We only stayed with Bill and Susan for a few days before we found a place to live by ourselves. It was an old house in Oregon City, a working class town south of Portland on the Eastern shore of the Willamette River. The house stood on a bluff above the decommissioned saw mill just downstream and had a beautiful view of the river. The house itself was a wooden structure with a wood burning stove. The bedroom was the attic, a large space with a sloping roof and a low ceiling. Bill could not have stood up in it, and even I, at 5 feet 8 inches, banged my head more than once.

The house came with some left-behind furniture. The first thing we bought for ourselves was a television set at an estate sale. It was an old black and white in a beautiful wood cabinet. It was by far the nicest piece of furniture we owned—although the TV did not work too well. We had bought it to watch one program--"Kung Fu."

Kung Fu was an "Eastern Western" that depicted the adventures of Quai Chang Caine, a Chinese/Caucasian Shaolin Priest who is exiled from China and lands in the Western United States in the post Civil War Era. It was on for three seasons (1972-1975). The themes of racism and the oppression of the weak by the strong ran through the show, as well as the uses and limitations of force as a means of confronting evil. We loved it.

We came upon an ad for a Kung Fu studio in the local alternative weekly. At that time karate and judo were the Asian martial art forms known to Americans. There was some awareness of Kung Fu because of the TV show, but Ti Chi was completely unknown.

We went to the studio. The teacher was a young Chinese man from Hawaii. He explained that his uncle, who was a grand-master, had sent him to the mainland to see if it would be possible to teach this practice to non-Chinese. Kevin was a remarkable character. When he was not teaching, he was a typical American jock. He had played football in college, smoked cigarettes and seemed totally "American." When he put on his robe and dimmed the lights in the small dojo space, it was as if he was channeling his grand-master uncle. He spoke in aphorisms and moved at the speed of light—or so it seemed. I can still vividly recall the time he was standing in front of us and then was standing behind our backs. We had never seen him make the transition.

This was our introduction to "Chi"—the Eastern concept of the universal energy that flows through all things. It is the life force that keeps us alive, and its healthy flow is the basis of Chinese medicine. The principles of yin and yang are connected to it, and those who understand how to work with it are capable of things that seem impossible. I remember a long conversation between Rachael and myself about the miracles described in the New Testament, and how they might be understood as a supreme ability to control the Chi flowing through the world.

Kevin's main instruction was "slow becomes fast and fast becomes slow." What this meant for the training process was that one needed to stand in the "Ma," or horse position, for hours on end in order to build a firm base for all the spectacular Kung Fu moves that would-be students had come to learn. It was an excruciating process, and I was amazed at how readily Rachael, who had never worked out before, was willing and able to stand so still for so long. I went with it, mostly in support for her and her enthusiasm, which was strong enough to suggest an important past life experience in an Eastern monastery.

One night, about four months into the training, we went to the dojo and found it closed. There was no sign on the door and nothing to tell us what was going on. We returned a few more times, but it was clear that our teacher was gone. Although we had not seen it coming, we were not surprised. Almost all the other students had drifted away. Americans did not seem ready for the discipline needed to master this form. We were done with Kung Fu, but we took with us the principle of "slow becomes fast..." and found it helpful in many situations over the years, especially in issues of children and their development. But we were now free—there was nothing to keep us in Portland. We could continue our quest, wherever it might lead us.

We began to talk about where we might go and what we might do next. As we were contemplating this a new obstacle arose in the form of Sam Gilbert, the "Godfather of UCLA Basketball" and the man who had negotiated Bill's contract with the Blazers.

THE SHADOW OF THE GODFATHER

Bill and Susan's house was a gathering place for the newly refurbished Portland Trailblazer basketball team, and their families. Sid Wicks had joined the team from UCLA, Geoff Petrie from Princeton and Lenny Wilkins was the player/coach. Bill had undergone surgery on his leg during the summer, and the team was anxious for him to play. At the time, it was routine in the NBA to rush players back into action after injuries and pump them full of pain killers and other medication to keep them on the court. Bill ended up missing more than half the games that first season due to injury, and even at that played much more than he should have. I have no doubt that this was a significant factor in shortening his career and adding to the chronic pain and disability that has remained long after his playing days came to an end.

Before Bill's joining the Trailblazers, Portland had been an unsuccessful NBA franchise on the court and off. Despite being the only major sport in town, the citizens of Portland were quite uninterested in Basketball. Portland was still, in many ways, a small and white town. Basketball was a sport dominated by black athletes, and it just was not popular in Portland. Attendance was low and interest the same. Here, again, Bill was something of a "great white hope." And, from the day of his arrival until the present day, the Trail-blazers have sold out every home game in every season—often televising games into other venues in order to provide a communal place for those who cannot get tickets to watch the games live at the stadium.

When we had arrived in Portland there was another couple staying with Bill and Susan, Jack and Micki Scott. Jack was already well known as a radical sports figure. He was a track coach and had been involved with John Carlos and Tommy Smith, the two American track stars who raised their arms in the Black Power salute while on the podium to receive their medals during the 1968 Summer Olympics. Now Jack and Micki were in Portland and living with Bill and Susan. They were suspicious of us and perhaps saw us as "competitors" for Bill's attention and influence, but once they realized that we had no such designs on Bill, we became very friendly.

One day, early in 1975, Jack appeared at our door. He said he was going away for a while, and that the FBI might come around looking for him. He was concerned that Bill's phone would be tapped because of him and said he would call us with messages. He also asked us to "watch out for Bill," since we were more politically experienced and knowledgeable. He then said goodbye and left. A few weeks later two FBI agents showed up at our door. They wanted to come in and ask questions. We inquired if they had either a search warrant or a subpoena. They did not, so we pointed down the hill and suggested they return with one or the other if they wanted to talk with us. They left and never came back. When Jack returned he gave Rachael a pair of paisley jeans covered with flowers that were too small for his wife, but which he thought might fit Rachael. Both of us had lost considerable weight on our new diet, but even so, Rachael could barely close the zipper. We later found out that the FBI suspected Jack of transporting Patricia Hearst from California to a farmhouse in Pennsylvania where she and other SLA members had hidden for a period. The jeans belonged to Patty.

On another morning Bill came to our door. Rachael and I were in the process of writing "The Pushers" and were in the habit of staying up all night and sleeping during the day. This hardly mattered as it was always dark and rainy, and day and night seemed to run together in the Portland gloom. We staggered out of bed and down the stairs to see who was knocking on our door so early in the day. When we saw Bill we opened the door and he said "I'm moving to Cuba to play for their National Team." We invited him in, made a cup of strong tea, and sat down to talk. We asked him why he wanted to do this and to consider the personal, professional and political implications of this move. We also pointed out that, like us when we wanted to go to Chile, he didn't speak Spanish either. He left and we never spoke of it again.

In March, the NCAA College basketball tournament had scheduled an early round to take place in Portland. Bill got tickets for the four of us for the games at the Portland Coliseum. As was our custom, none of us stood for the national anthem. During halftime, Bill pointed out that Sam Gilbert was seated a few rows above us and suggested that Rachael, who had brought her camera, should go and take a picture of Sam. We knew that Bill and Sam had broken off their association, but we did not realize the depth of their falling out. We also did not know that Sam was a former boxer, was built like a bull and had a violent temperament. When he saw Rachael standing at the end of the row with her camera, he came at her and shoved the camera into her face, bloodying and breaking her nose. The police came and took statements and a picture of Bill with Rachael and me was on the front page of the Oregonian the next day, along with a statement from Sam that he had "no choice" as he feared Rachael was attacking him. The picture showed a small (around 100 lbs), 20-year-old woman between Bill and myself, looking even smaller in contrast to the two of us.

We met with the district attorney, who declined to prosecute Sam for his assault. We also spoke to a law firm about pressing civil charges against him. They were willing to take the case, but pointed out that this was Portland, not LA, and that a jury was not going to award big money in the same way that a big-city jury might. The witnesses they had interviewed mainly remembered us as the people who had not stood for the anthem, and were less clear on the details of the confrontation. The lawyers also said that the case would probably drag on for some time, as Sam had plenty of resources and would undoubtedly use delaying tactics in any legal situation. Still, they were willing to go forward if we wanted them to. They agreed that his bullying behavior was outrageous, and were happy to work with us to see him brought to account.

By this time Rachael and I had decided that we wanted to go out into the desert. We had the idea that we would do a long term cleansing fast and perhaps experience a vision that would reveal the next step on our journey. Were we willing to postpone our quest in order to pursue the case against Sam?

The "old" Rachael, the feisty New York fighter, would stay and make sure Sam got what was coming to him-regardless of the size of any settlement. The "new" spiritual Rachael wondered if this was not a distraction and a test of her dedication to walking a new path. Included in the mix was that things were quite difficult for Bill and Susan at the time. Bill had missed most of the season due to injury, and he was coming under extreme criticism from some fans and sportswriters who questioned his commitment to the team and basketball itself. They would be dragged into any lawsuit, which would be a big front page story in a small city like Portland, and keep the media spotlight on Bill in an uncomfortable way. In the end, Rachael decided to not pursue the case. Her nose hurt under certain conditions for years afterward, but she never felt she had made a mistake by walking away.

We made our plans to leave. We sold the old square-back and bought a VW Bus, took out the middle seat and put in a bed and storage space. We held a "writers' liquidation sale" and got rid of our books, the mimeograph and lots of other things. All money was converted to $100 bills rolled up in a small, 35mm film can. Rachael sewed us "Kung Fu" outfits and capes. We put some of our things in Bill and Susan's basement, but took our favorite picture out of its frame, rolled it up and put it in a tube to take with us. It was an original oil painting that we had spotted while living in Venice and walking down the Boardwalk during an art fair. It depicted a lush green fantasy landscape with a maiden in the foreground, staring across the water at the towers of a mystical city. Rachael had loved it when we first saw it. I hurried her away and came back alone to buy it for her. I paid $50, which was a lot—to me—at the time. We have had it ever since, and it has graced the bedroom of every place we have ever lived.

On the first sunny day we had seen in Portland, immediately after the Memorial day weekend of 1975, we loaded our few possessions and our faithful dog Emma into our VW van and left the Northwest for the Arizona desert and whatever revelations it might bring.

THE SPEAR OF DESTINY

We headed South out of Portland on Highway 5, cutting over to the 101 in order to visit friends in San Francisco and Berkeley before turning East on Interstate 80 to Salt Lake City and then south to Arizona. We were in no particular hurry and open to whatever adventures might await us.

Even though we had sold or stored everything we owned, we still could not resist the lure of a good used bookstore, and The Bay Area had more than its share. So it was that one evening we found ourselves browsing through books again. I was in the history section when I came across a paperback that purported to unveil the secret of Hitler's fascination with the occult, and how it had affected his rise and fall. It looked interesting, but I resisted the temptation to purchase and moved on to Literature. Several minutes later I heard Rachael calling my name from across the store.

"Abraham, take a look at this." She was standing in the History department, waving a book at me. It was *The Spear of Destiny*, the same volume I had picked up and put back. We took it to the checkout counter, paid our $2, and left the store. The next morning we continued on our trek to the desert.

We saw some beautiful country, staying mostly at camp-sites and sleeping in our converted van. We took turns driving, listening to our favorite Rock, Soul, Folk and Blues record-ings on the cassettes we had collected. This new format, which had entered the market in the early 1970's, allowed us to bring our music with us when we traveled, eliminating the need to navigate through the country, commercial pop and evangelists who dominated the airways outside of major metropolitan areas. We played the 1973 recording of Sonny Terry and Brownie McGhee that included "On the Road Again" over and over, and it was the first CD we bought when that format replaced cassettes.

We talked endlessly about everything, or else one of us would lie in the back reading or resting while the other drove. And we met many old men, hitch hiking on these back roads, convinced they were prophets come again to wander the des-erts and speak their truths. We listened to their stories and dropped them off with a $10 bill to buy their next meal or room for the night.

When we got to Salt Lake City we changed into our Kung Fu clothes and visited the great Mormon Tabernacle. It was certainly an impressive structure. The whole city was amazing to us. We had never seen any place so clean and so white—especially the people. We were constantly asked, in a polite way, what cult we were part of. We always replied, "None-it's just the two of us." They would just look at us quizzically and move along. We left after just a few hours and began the southward leg of our journey.

I had begun reading *The Spear of Destiny* a few days earlier. The Spear in question was the one carried by the Roman soldier who had pierced the side of Christ as he was dying on the Cross. By doing this, according to legend, it had become imbued with a certain cosmic power. The person who had possession of the Spear would be very powerful, and, according to the Author, Hitler was obsessed with finding and owning this instrument. He also was said to be part of a circle of Black Magicians, integrating Eastern and Western approaches to gaining access to these dark secrets.

In the course of the story, Trevor Ravenscroft, the author, dropped in the name "Rudolf Steiner." According to Ravenscroft, Steiner was a German philosopher and mystic who was "the only one who recognized the depth of Hitler's evil," seeing him for who he was, even as early as the early 1920's. He went on to say that Steiner had access to the "Akashic Record," a spiritual script upon which all human history was inscribed. I had never heard of Steiner, but I was fascinated as I lay in the back of the van, heading down the two lane highway through the mountains towards the Arizona desert. Suddenly, the van stopped. Rachael called out to me "Abraham, come up here quick." I jumped off the bed and hurried to the front of van. There, in the middle of the road, sat a huge hawk, blocking our way forward.

"Don't you know what this means?" I cried.

"It means we have to change our path. Birds are the messengers of the gods, and they are sending us a message to go somewhere else."

As soon as I finished saying this, the hawk flew away, leaving us parked in the middle of the fortunately deserted mountain road. We pulled over to the side. I told Rachael about what I had been reading, and we decided to go to Los Angeles to visit her parents, whom we had not seen since we had left for Portland, and also to see if we could find out more about this Rudolf Steiner person. We took a right turn and headed West, back to Venice where our journey had begun.

When we got to Southern California we did some research and discovered that there was a group dedicated to Steiner and his work. It was called the "Anthroposophical Society," with international headquarters in Switzerland and a national office in New York. We called New York and they gave us a number for the "Rudolf Steiner Library" in upstate New York. When we spoke to the Librarian he said that they did send books out by mail, but also that there was a Library in Los Angeles and gave us the phone number. The next day we found ourselves on Normandie Ave. in the mid-Wilshire District, just west of downtown LA, standing in front of an older house with a an odd-shaped sign that read "Anthroposophical Society of Los Angeles" in a kind of thick Germanic Font.

We knocked on the door and were greeted by a kindly looking older man—the one with whom we had spoken on the phone. His name was Richard (Dick) Betteridge and he was the volunteer Librarian. He led us upstairs to the Library itself. It was quite a large room with bookcases along all the walls, and all the cases filled with volumes written by Rudolf Steiner or people working out of his inspiration. There were also several smaller rooms filled with most of the same books, only in the original German. Dick told us that Steiner had written 20 books and given over 8000 lectures, and it was the lectures that comprised the vast majority of the volumes we saw. He told us that "Anthroposophy" meant the wisdom (Sophia) of the human being (Anthro). He also told us that Steiner had a PhD in Science and described his approach as "Spiritual Science," fusing two world conceptions that are generally regarded as at odds with each other.

It was overwhelming. I asked him for the specific title that Ravenscroft had referred to in *The Spear of Destiny*. It was called *The Fifth Gospel*—referring to the one written in the Akashic Record rather than the four contained in the Standard version of the New Testament. I took it back to where we were staying and quickly devoured it. I finished with a glazed look on my face. I had hardly understood a word of it. I had no idea what he was talking about.

The last time I had felt like this was in college, when faced with the work of certain academic sociologists whose work was so densely filled with jargon, it was impossible to penetrate. In that instance I had come to the (correct) conclusion that this was an attempt to create a vocabulary available only to the initiated professionals to help them maintain control over their terrain. They were using big words to describe things that could be explained more simply, and building complex edifices to mask the shallowness of their observations.

I understood that my experience with Steiner was different. The phenomena, and his approach to it, was outside of my experience and I was going to have to learn a new language in order to penetrate a discipline wholly foreign to me. I found a couple of his basic works and we continued to browse the shelves, as was our habit when surrounded by books.

While I was examining titles and blurbs, Rachael was proceeding in her more intuitive fashion, letting her eyes and hands roam over the volumes until one compelled her to pull it off the shelf. She looked it over and brought it to me. It was a slim pamphlet with the strange title, *The Influences of Lucifer and Ahriman*. The first name was familiar to me, but I had never heard of the second. I had the feeling that it might address good and evil, a subject I had been thinking about all my life. Being born into a Jewish family right after the second world war, as we both had been, made this a question of immediate and more than academic interest. We were constantly reminded, in one way or another, that six million of our people had been captured, enslaved, tortured and executed by an advanced European nation only a few years ago. The State of Israel had been founded to provide a haven for the Jewish People, to ensure that this never happened again. We had watched dogs being let loose on black people who wanted to ride on a bus, drink out of a water fountain or eat at a lunch counter as if they were regular human beings. We had watched our own country drop millions of tons of bombs on peasants and their homes 10,000 miles away from us and I had been told that I needed to participate in that action to protect my country and its way of life. The whole world seemed to be ruled by evil. Henry Kissinger's Nobel Peace prize was the ultimate symbol of this state of affairs. We were more than curious about what Rudolf Steiner could add to our understanding of this burning question that had lived in our souls for so long.

Within the first page he had given us a whole new understanding of good and evil—one that became obvious and obviously true as soon as it was pointed out. There are, he said, two kinds of evil—hot and cold. We all intuitively know and recognize this. Even the law differentiates between crimes of passion, carried out in the "heat of the moment," and "cold blooded murder," often connected with money and involving calculation and planning. The former are crimes of the heart, the latter crimes of the head. Steiner identified one spiritual being he called "Lucifer" with the force of hot evil and the other, the being of cold materialist thinking, he called Ahriman. The being that balances the two he called "Christ."

I was reminded of the image of the circle of life presented in Chinese Medicine and in Kung Fu, the two halves with dots in the center of each, separated by a wavy line. Yin and Yang, the hot and cold elements that must be balanced for health, with the wavy line of the Tao—the Way—just as Christ described himself as "The Way, the Truth and the Life." The whole dualistic paradigm dissolved, replaced by a world severely out of balance, with the force of Love, by whatever name, as the power that was available to help us bring about the healing the world was crying out for.

Of course there was, and is, much more to the question. But the basic insight and approach has remained a key element for penetrating events in the inner and outer world, and has continued to inform my understanding of how to approach politics and social transformation.

As I continued to read Steiner, I became convinced that he was answering my "Sunday School" question about the nature of the human being—the "ape versus angel" debate that I had for so long felt was the fundamental question in my life. His approach satisfied me both intellectually and intuitively—it had the ring of truth that reverberates in both head and heart.

What was most amazing was that Rachael felt the same. It was not one of us "pulling" the other into this new direction. We both recognized Steiner, and our connection to him and his work. We both felt this to be the new path we needed to walk. And we both jumped on to the path with both feet. But first we had to complete the journey into the desert we had begun in Portland. We loaded ourselves and Emma into the van and headed out to Arizona in the midst of the summer. We went into a small bank on the outskirts of Scottsdale, dressed in our Kung Fu garb, rented a safe deposit box for our film can of cash and a few other valuables and headed out into the mountainous desert country with a few water bottles and a couple of sleeping bags, plus some food for the dog.

We lasted three days. There was no water that we could find, the sun was relentless, and we got really hungry. We came back to the bank, retrieved our valuables and headed once again to Santa Barbara and the ocean.

I'M GETTIN' MARRIED
IN THE MORNING

When we returned to Santa Barbara we once again needed to find a place to live. By now our money was getting lower and we had to consider our options. We decided to visit the Sunburst Community above the city to see if a communal setting of spiritual seekers might be something we could connect to. The setting was lovely and the people were friendly. They told us we could spend the night there, but said that as we were not married, we could not stay in the same cabin. We thought this was very strange and decided to end our visit right after dinner.

On our way down the mountain we ran out of gas. As we sat by a creek along the side of the road and waited for help to arrive, we discussed what had happened at Sunburst. Neither Rachael nor myself had ever considered marriage. We saw no need to involve the State in our relationship. This was between us, and we did not need their sanction. Now we began to wonder whether there might be some spiritual significance to the "formalization" of our relationship in conjunction with the larger community in which we were embedded. By the time help arrived, we were engaged.

We quickly found a wonderful place to rent. It was the lower level of a large house on the cliffs of Goleta, just north of Santa Barbara and south of UC Santa Barbara in Isla Vista. The view was of a magnificent rose garden cultivated by the owner of the house, who was a retired diplomat. Beyond the Rose Garden was the Pacific Ocean stretching out to infinity. It could not have been more beautiful. The only problem was that we could not move in for two weeks, and had to find a cheap place to stay in the meantime.

We settled in the Modoc. The Modoc might have been called a flea-bag motel, but unfortunately it was tics rather than fleas that came with the territory. We spent much of time pulling these disgusting creatures off of Emma's skin, and sometimes our own. We felt this was the purgatory we needed to endure while waiting to enter the heaven of our hilltop home on the ridge. In the meantime, we planned our weddings.

We knew that we needed to do something "different." Not for the sake of being different, but just because we were different and would not be happy with a traditional wedding. At the same time, we wanted to please our families and acknowledge them, as well as include our friends in the occasion. In the end, we decided we would have three weddings: one for just us, one with our friends, and one with our families. When we told Rachael's folks we were getting married, their first question was "Are you pregnant?" We were kind of shocked but said "no, we're not. We want to celebrate our commitment to each other." We did not tell them our plan for the three marriage ceremonies, but told then that we wanted a small wedding just with our families. We knew that Irv White sometimes put his rabbi clothes on to perform weddings, and we asked him if he would do this for us. He was delighted.

We scouted locations. For ourselves we found a small cave right on the beach near our place. We would have some shelter from the wind and could do the ceremony under the stars. We also found a wonderful spot in the hills above Malibu. It was called the "Escondido Canyon Retreat Center." There was a small lake with a grassy area where a ceremony and small reception could take place. We decided to hold both of the public ceremonies there. Hank Babcock would officiate at the one for our friends, which would take place a week before the family wedding.

It was a magical time for us. We took a walk up State Street in Santa Barbara and went into a small jewelry store. The jeweler was an older man. We told him that we were getting married and could not afford to spend much on wedding bands. He asked us how much we could afford and we told him "twenty-five dollars for each ring." He bent down and took matching bands of gold, embossed with hearts, and showed them to us. "How about these?," He asked. They were beautiful, and we knew that they really sold for much more. When we returned after the weddings to thank him again, his son was in the store. He told us that his father had died in the interim. It was likely that giving us these rings was one of his final transactions in the store he had owned and operated for much of his life.

On Main St. in Santa Monica we went into a shop that specialized in imports from India and found matching white outfits. In a store full of expensive goods, these beautiful caftans were the least expensive items on the clothing rack. There were only two—one in Rachael's size and one in mine. At this time we were still eating a fruit based diet and fasting 2 or 3 days a week. Both of us were at our lowest weight since childhood, and neither of us would ever fit into our wedding dresses again.

When we went to the Courthouse in Santa Barbara to get our license, we were told that blood tests were necessary. This was almost a deal breaker, as Rachael hated getting blood drawn and was likely to faint during the process. We found a friendly judge who gave us a waiver.

During our nighttime ceremony on the beach, the waves came up into the cave and washed away our custom made sandals. We accepted this as a sacrifice to the sea gods for their blessing on our union and vowed to always return to the ocean on our anniversary, a vow we have kept for more than forty years.

The ceremony with our friends was somewhat surreal. We had not seen almost any of them since we had left Los Angeles a little over a year before. Here we were, in our matching dresses, getting married by a friend who had written his own ceremony calling upon the angels to bless our union. Hank's girlfriend, Barbara, gave us a stone in the shape of a heart that she had found. We have it to this day.

Our other friends hardly knew what to make of us, but they could recognize our love for each other and the energy that flowed between us. It was the last time we saw almost any of these people from our former lives, and really marked a new direction for us, as weddings often do.

We were doing the family wedding, with a Jewish ceremony, for the sake of our parents, and needed to find a balance between what appealed to us and what would make them happy. My parents came from Chicago and my Uncle Jay came all the way from Florida, bringing with him an expensive bottle of Scotch whiskey for the wedding toast.

We did not want to hold the wedding in a synagogue, but Irv White was happy to do an outdoor service at the retreat center. It was a remote spot and we had to carry the wedding canopy (called a "huppa" in Hebrew) and chairs from the parking lot to the grassy area more than 100 yards away. Even though it was warm, it was also windy, and it took four people to keep the canopy upright during the ceremony. Still, it was a beautiful place and a beautiful ceremony, and in the end everyone was glad they had made the winding drive through the coastal hills for this unique event that was certainly different than any wedding they had ever attended.

Finding a dinner venue had been a challenge. We had suggested "The Golden Temple of Conscious Cookery," a restaurant owned and operated by a Eastern religious sect. When Rachael's dad came with us to check it out, we met with the Yogi himself. Irv pulled out a cigarette and the Yogi told him there was no smoking in the restaurant, at which point Irv said that we could not have the dinner there and we left. He explained to us that he himself could have put up with this, but his older sister, who was coming all the way from Florida and was a heavy smoker, would have been very offended to be told she could not smoke during the meal.

Rachael's parents knew that serving steak or prime rib would gross us out, but they felt obligated to serve "real food" to their dinner guests. We ended up at a nice fish restaurant near Marina Del Rey, where Irv and Shirley were living at the time. Rachael and I had incredible fruit plates and everyone else had salmon and eyed our fruit plate with envy. Rachael's dad had gone all the way across the city to pick up our wedding cake, which was made of crushed almonds and dates as a base and had "love forever" spelled out in blueberries across the top.

Since we did not have a place to live and did not eat any cooked foods, people were forced to give us money as a wedding gift. This was great, as we had by then gone through almost all of Rachael's small inheritance and my game show winnings. Now we had enough to live on for another few months, while figuring out the next steps on the new path we had chosen—or that had chosen us.

The ceremony with families took place on July 27, 1975. It was less than nine years since I had walked away from Yale Law School with no idea of who I was or what I was going to do. I was married to my soul mate, in the healthiest condition of my life, with a clear spiritual path before me and with confidence that no matter what challenges the future might bring, I would be able to face them. After all, I was Abraham. One year later to the day, our first child, Jubilee, was born in a cabin among the hills of Cazadero, an hour and half north of San Francisco in rural Sonoma County. But that, of course, is another story...

ABOUT THE AUTHOR

Abraham Entin is a singer, songwriter, and storyteller who dances at every opportunity. He is a long-time student of Rudolf Steiner's social ideas and is particularly interested in how spiritual perspectives influence and help bring about positive social change. After the events described in this memoir, Abraham and his wife Rachael Flug went on to create Diaperaps, Ltd., a business that helped revitalize cloth diapering for the benefit of babies and the environment. He founded the Sonoma County affiliate of Move to Amend and has written extensively on corporate personhood, money, and debt. He received a certificate of appreciation from Occupy Santa Rosa for his "tireless support of the Occupy Movement and his work to end corporate greed and corruption." Rachael and Abraham live an hour north of San Francisco in western Sonoma County. They have three wonderful adult children and two fabulous grandchildren, all of whom bring great joy to their lives. At seventy-three, Abraham is still out rousing the rabble. His website is www.LeversofPower.org, where you can hear his music, read other works, and find out how to bring him to your community for a performance.